Che Bella Figura!

SUNY series in Speech Communication
Dudley Cahn, Editor

and

SUNY series in Italian/American Studies
Fred L. Gardaphe, Editor

Gloria Nardini

Che Bella Figura!

THE POWER
OF PERFORMANCE
IN AN ITALIAN LADIES' CLUB
IN CHICAGO

STATE UNIVERSITY
OF NEW YORK PRESS

Published by
State University of New York Press

© 1999 State University of New York

Printed in the United States of America

For information, address the State University of New York Press,
State University Plaza, Albany, NY 12246

Marketing by Anne Valentine • Production by Bernadine Dawes

Library of Congress Cataloging-in-Publication Data

Nardini, Gloria, 1942-
    Che bella figura! : the power of performance in an Italian
ladies' club in Chicago / Gloria Nardini.
        p. cm. — (SUNY series in speech communication) (SUNY series
in Italian/American studies)
    Includes bibliographical references and index.
    ISBN 0-7914-4091-5 (alk. paper)
    ISBN 0-7914-4092-3 (pbk. : alk. paper)
    1. Italian American women—Illinois—Chicago—Societies and
clubs. 2. Italian American women—Illinois—Chicago—Social
conditions. 3. Italian Americans—Illinois—Chicago—Social life
and customs. 4. Chicago (Ill.)—Social life and customs. I. Title.
II. Series. III. Series: SUNY series in Italian/American studies
    E184.I8 N4 1999
    305.48'851073—dc21
                                    99-19064
                                    CIP

1   2   3   4   5   6   7   8   9   10

CONTENTS

Preface   vii
Acknowledgments ix

My Methodology: The Ethnography of   1
Communication

ONE   5
A Definition of *Bella Figura*

TWO   35
The Conceptual Framework of this Study and
Related Literature on Women's Language

THREE   55
A History of the Collandia Club

FOUR   77
Bella Figura at the Collandia Club

FIVE   105
The Transcript: A Linguistic Event Transformed
by *Bella Figura*

Conclusion   127
Appendix A   133
Endnotes   143
Works Cited   149
Index   159

PREFACE

My first real comprehension of the concept of *bella figura* came after I had been a participant observer for some months in the Collandia Club. As the recording secretary, it was my job to take minutes and then read them back at the next meeting, so I dutifully tape recorded everything and took notes. But nothing ever seemed to happen. Committee chairwomen would be praised, birthdays would be announced, we would play Bingo, eat cake and coffee, and then it was all over. It seemed so boring that I was beginning to wonder how I would ever find anything to write about!

One evening, however, a discussion occurred in which several officers took issue with the validity of the treasurer's report. While their presentations of difference were not adversarial, they were—clearly and forcefully—in disagreement both with the treasurer and with each other. Other members, too, added their opinions to the general melee. My ears perked up. Finally, I thought, something was happening at this Collandia Club meeting! Excitedly, I took notes and wondered about how I would analyze them later. Had I found an underlying source of tension which had heretofore been hidden? Who would "win" this argument? Would there be hard feelings? While the issue itself was not resolved right then, it was clear to me that I was finally seeing a real meeting!

That next morning, Toni, one of my principal informants, telephoned. "I think it's awful," she said, "for officers to disagree like that at a meeting. They can say what they want to each other beforehand, but at the meeting in front of the members, they should be united." I was stunned. Enculturated into the notion of meeting-as-an-appropriate-site-for-contention, I viewed arguing there as legitimate. But Toni clearly had a different definition of "meeting" than I did. Apparently, she thought of it as a performance, a presentation. Her Italian, *"presentarsi unite,"* literally translates as "present themselves united." So for Toni a meeting defined itself as a playing-out-of-appropriate-roles by the officers in front of the general membership. Anything other than this presentation of unity she found in poor taste, almost disgraceful.

This was for me a moment of epiphany. From it came my gut-level understanding of *bella figura* and this book.

ACKNOWLEDGMENTS

To my family—my father Augustus J. Lazzerini, my sister Joan, my husband Francesco (who created the pseudonym "Collandia" and drew my maps), my sons Gian Carlo and Guido—go appreciation for their loving support of their daughter, sister, wife, mother, respectively. My sister was especially instrumental in helping me realize the important role that *bella figura* played in our growing up. I thank her for listening carefully by telephone—whether she wanted to or not—to every word of every rough draft of every chapter. And then to the revisions.

To my dissertation committee, Marcia Farr, Margherita Pieracci Harwell, Elliot Judd, Richard Cameron, and Christian Messenger, go thanks for their helpful suggestions and for the hours they spent reading my chapters. I am especially grateful to Marcia Farr, whose absolute commitment to the ethnography of communication inspired me in the first place. Her gentle comments—spare but salient—pushed me to consider and reconsider my analysis until I was sure that it would meet with her intellectual approval.

I am also grateful for the interest of Professoressa Margherita Pieracci Harwell, whose subtle native understandings of the ways of *bella figura* greatly enriched my appreciation of it. Always kind and encouraging, she gave hours and hours of taped interview time to help me shape what I wanted to say.

Others extended helping hands: Betty Boyd, Molly Loeser, and Lee Horning doggedly pursued books and articles; Bill Fowler solved computer problems; Norine Bertagni commented perceptively on each draft; Marisa Bonaccorsi served as translator par excellence. The Immigration History Research Center at the University of Minnesota allowed me access to works I would never have been able to read otherwise. Bill Covino's guidance helped me interest the State University of New York Press in my

manuscript. Fred Gardaphe and Sabina Magliocco read and commented on revised drafts of my first chapter.

I thank the Collandia Ladies, whose hospitality and joie de
vivre make the hours I spend with them a pleasure. I shall never
forget their enthusiasm on the day in which "Dr." appeared in
front of my name for the first time. They congratulated me as if
they had had a stake in it all—which, of course, they had.

Finally, *Che Bella Figura* is dedicated to Mary Ber, who gave
of herself emotionally and intellectually in unimaginable ways,
making the book her project almost as much as mine.

My Methodology: The Ethnography
of Communication

I joined the Collandia Ladies' Club in the summer of 1991. As the wife of a Collandia member and the daughter of a father who is a respected Italian American community leader, I have a kind of birthright of entitlement to this club. The first time I entered I was warmly welcomed by a woman of my father's generation who introduced me as her *paesana* ("woman from the same town"). I had never thought of myself before as anyone's *paesana*.

I am also a feminist. As I set out to do ethnography, I became a participant observer, going to monthly meetings and joining the bocce team. My initial plan was to study how Italian and English functioned to make gender issues "learned" rather than "natural," but I felt increasingly uncomfortable about whether or not my initial proposal was viable. Any gender issues which I was seeing—and they virtually jumped off the pages of my field notes—seemed a matter of unconcern for most Collandia Ladies. The issue of second-class citizenship in this club seemed not an "emic" one, and to focus on it, therefore, not in accordance with the principles of ethnography. I told myself that I needed to keep an open mind. I continued to "hang out" and take notes.

My activities within the Club intensified, as more was asked of me—especially when my literacy in English and Italian became common knowledge. I was recording secretary and for two years I taped meetings, wrote minutes, and read them aloud at each meeting. When there were official letters to write, especially asking for donations, I wrote them. I interviewed various members and wrote profiles of them for the Club newsletter; I also wrote

1

movie reviews and reports of social outings; I helped translate the (men's) club president's messages from Italian to English.

Committee work also began to take up major amounts of time as my research became more long-term. I was co-chair of the 1992 fashion show and on the committees of the '93 and '94 shows; specifically, I found raffle gifts and coordinated the evening's events. I also put together a "how to" folder on the fashion show which was passed on to the new chairwomen. I served on the Christmas Party Committee twice, creating formats for the program and writing speeches for the President. I made gifts for the Christmas Bazaar and helped sell them.

I received countless phone calls from Toni, one of the unofficial leaders of the Club whose job it is to take phone reservations and seat people for the assorted functions. She has done so for over twenty years. At Toni's behest, I bought Christmas and birthday gifts for the men's and ladies' club presidents. I also realized that our phone conversations, besides serving the function of indoctrinating me into Club lore, had another purpose: I was supposed to convey her shrewd messages about how the club functioned to my friend, the President, who spoke only English. (Toni, who had immigrated to Chicago in her thirties, was more comfortable expressing herself in Italian.) This realization allowed me to contextualize events which heretofore I had been observing helter-skelter. Thus, Toni served not only as an important principal informant, but also as someone with whom I could triangulate my data to reach an "emic" perspective. She was always right.

For all of the above events, I took extensive field notes. Sometimes I tape-recorded officers' and/or committee meetings; I took notes on all thirty-one tapes, completely transcribing three. I interviewed many members (informally because setting up formal interviews did not seem to work—people gave me "official" answers) on the origins of the club, the meaning of *bella figura*, the way club business has always been handled, women's opinions on the current arguments, etc. I read both the ladies' club minutes for the last six years and all of the old newsletters which I was able to find. I carefully examined sets of bylaws, those of the men and those of the women. I tried to pay particular attention to social and political structures within the Ladies' Club, especially to issues of power. Gradually, I began to re-evaluate my sense of the blatant sexism which I observed when I came. I needed to understand the subtle ways in which many of the women dealt with it or chose to ignore it.

I have read and re-read my field notes, writing analysis notes which attempt to make sense of them. I kept a log in which to record my insights. I also have depended upon personal introspection for my conclusions. In particular, I have analyzed my ongoing participation in my Italian family (during yearly visits to Lucca) which allows me a holistic sense of the culture. Discussions with my native-born Italian husband and my American-born sister have confirmed my intuitions about what it means to be Lucchese and what it means to be Lucchese-American.

If it's true that all writing is autobiographical, then this book is too, for in researching the Collandia Club, I have had to suppress my first reaction to every problem I encountered. By nature and socialization into American culture, I am forthright and direct, but I learned the value of indirection as a coping strategy which the Collandia ladies more frequently employ. I have had to acknowledge the importance of "feminine touches" to the social amenities of everyday living. I have had to reassess my entire life's experiences in order to really comprehend how all-encompassing *bella figura* is. As a phrase in Italian, I have always known it—frequently used it in speech, in fact—but only now do I appreciate the depth to which it functions in the culture. I have always relied heavily on my intellectual powers, but to enter into the Collandia, I had to discard them as my traditional tools, for *bella figura* isn't about logic. It's about feelings. And it matters above all.

Some issues remain unresolved. Where does feminism fit in, for example? Italian feminism, so different from American feminism, disdains political equality with men but seeks instead to create "the politics of relations" as a "practice" among women. According to theorist Luisa Muraro, it is a "story, not a reasoned argument." Does this "story" emerge at the Collandia? Are these women—without realizing it, of course—Italian feminists? I don't know. I do know that understanding *bella figura* helped me to understand their power. In retrospect, I realize it was something I knew about even before I started my research.

What I have most gradually realized as I fixated on problems of order in the writing of this book—where should I put my epiphany? my definitions? where should the review of the litera-ture go?—is that we are all products of our own culture. No rhetoric is ever neutral; and ethnography is the rhetoric I have employed to fix in time, and forever, two and one half years of the Collandia Club. This is the culture I come from. I hope to have done it justice. I hope to have made *bella figura*.

ONE

A Definition of *Bella Figura*

There exists in Italian an expression called *fare figura*, more frequently *fare bella figura*, whose literal meaning may be translated as "to make a beautiful figure." It is sometimes used to explain the Italian national character to non-Italians. For example, *Eyewitness Travel Guides* warns English-speaking tourists that "the skill of *fare bella figura* ('looking good') is so prized that visitors will be judged by the same standard"; it shows the figure of a slim, fashionable woman, her stylish purse slung over one shoulder. Underneath her lies the caption "Italian chic . . . *bella figura*" (19). Another publication, *Doing Business Abroad*, announces:

> Italians love style; in fact they live by it. *Bella figura* is no small part of their view of the world. Business negotiators tend to dress smartly, groom themselves neatly, and occupy modern well-equipped offices. . . . They make entrances and exits with a flourish, eat and drink well (but not excessively—so watch your drinking . . .) and talk about their families with pride. (Kennedy 172)

In order to teach this idiom in the context of appropriate situation and vocabulary, a recent advertisement for an Italian grammar textbook designed for American use prominently displays *BELLA FIGURA!* as one of its chapter titles. British journalist Charles Richards, who purports to explain the "new" Italians, defines "the cult of *bella figura* . . . [as] showing oneself off to one's best advantage" (57). Historian John Julius Norwich writes, "The Italians are extroverts, and acutely conscious of what others think of them. To make a *bella figura* is, and always has been since the days of ancient Rome, of primary importance; a *brutta figura* (an ugly figure), by contrast, is to be avoided at all costs" (28).

A search of the Internet (using the browser Netscape and search engines Excite, Infoseek, Lycos, and Yahoo) reveals numerous entries under *bella figura*. Lynn O'Hare contrasts the Italian outlook toward reality with that of Americans by discussing the concept of *bella figura*:

> Again and again, ITALIANS explained La Bella Figura to me as an overdeveloped concern with façade, the elaborate picture you show the world, and even a funny form of self-knowledge; unlike we Americans, compulsively mucking around in our inner selves, searching for MEANING and BEAUTY and VALUE there, the Italians cynically surmise maybe there's not a lot to be mined in that vein, and who really wants to? So LOOK GOOD, STRUT IT, FLAUNT IT—NOW! and leave what's inside, inside! <http://made-in-italy.com/fashion/newsl/lynn/htm>

In Italian texts, however, little explanation seems to be made of the term *bella figura*. Three recent publications that purport to describe *l'identitá degli italiani* (Italian identity) do not use it, even though they write about specifically Italian cultural constructs such as *mafioso* and *campanilismo* and *la dolce vita*.[1] Yet the notion of *bella figura* informs descriptions of Italian life. For example, without specifically naming them as *bella figura* traits, Ruggiero Romano calls "*mangiare e bere, bestemmiare e sentire magico, un certo gusto estetico o il piacere della vita in piazza*" ("eating and drinking, swearing and feeling magic, a certain aesthetic sense or the pleasure of life in public") elements common to all Italians, despite regional differences (*Paese Italia* xvii).

Italians writing about Italian life in English also seem not to make specific mention of *bella figura*. For example, journalist Luigi Barzini, author of *The Italians: A Full-Length Portrait Featuring Their Manners and Morals*, never uses the term although he gives an apt description of it. In his chapter on the importance of spectacle,

Barzini says, "This reliance on symbols and spectacles must be clearly grasped if one wants to understand Italy, Italian history, manners, civilization, habits. . . . It is the fundamental trait of the national character" (90).

Despite its seeming absence in the sociological and anthropological literature written by Italians themselves, the concept of *bella figura* is facilitated and emphasized by the language's habitual use of adjectival suffixes. Called *nomi alterati* ("altered nouns"), these suffixes create *sfumature* ("nuances") of subtle distinction (Fontanesi and Ugolotti 144). In the case of *figura* the following apply:

1. *figuraccia* in which the *dispregiativo* or "depreciatory" suffix "*accia*" means "bad";
2. *figurone* in which the *accrescitivo* or "augmentative" suffix "*one*" means "big", which implies "good";
3. *figurina* or *figuretta* or *figuruccia* in which the *diminutivo* or "diminisher" suffix *ina* or *etta* or *uccia* means "poor" or "measley".

In addition, by affixing an "s" to the verb *figurare* and creating *sfigurare*, the opposite meaning is achieved: not to make the figure.[2]

My contention is that *bella figura* is a central metaphor of Italian life, admittedly an extremely complicated one. It is a construct that refers to face, looking good, putting on the dog, style, appearance, flair, showing off, ornamentation, etiquette, keeping up with the Joneses, image, illusion, esteem, social status, reputation—in short, self-presentation and identity, performance and display. Further, I contend (with Lakoff and Johnson)[3] that as a cultural code it is deeply embedded as one of the primary arbiters of Italian social mores, so deeply imbedded that natives are frequently unaware (consciously at least) of conforming to it. But understanding Italian life is impossible without understanding the intensity with which one must *fare bella figura*.[4]

The term defies easy translation, making it perhaps even more important to attempt one, for, as Salman Rushdie advises his readers, "To unlock a society, look at its untranslatable words" (Burke, *Fortunes* 9). *Bella figura* is one such "word" in Italian. Dictionaries cite a variety of contexts for its use. *Il Nuovo Dizionario Italiano Garzanti*, published in 1984 in Milan, defines *far figura* as "*essere appariscente*" ("to be showy or striking, remarkable") and "*dare una buona impressione, apparire migliore della realtá*" ("to give a good impression, to appear better than the reality") (610). However, the term is usually construed as *far(e) bella figura*, literally "to make a beautiful figure." (Note that sometimes the final "*e*" of the infinitive "*fare*" is dropped). Garzanti says *far bella figura* means "*riuscire bene; ottenere apprezzamento e stima*" ("to make a beautiful figure" means "to succeed well; to obtain appreciation and respect") (611). Its opposite exists as well, namely *fare brutta figura*, literally "to make an ugly figure." There is also *fare cattiva figura*, in which *cattiva* translates as "bad," a slightly stronger indictment than *brutta*. For example, someone who eats with his hands makes a *brutta figura* whereas someone who refuses to help his infirm father to eat his soup makes a *cattiva figura*.[5]

Clearly, *far(e) figura* is too complicated a notion to be captured by a single dictionary definition, but the fact that the construct is well demonstrated in the Italian language demonstrates its importance in the culture. Many are its ramifications. Clothing can be the subject of the verb: *un vestito che fa figura* ("a showy dress"). In this case the emphasis is on appearance. Performance can also be emphasized. One can *far figura nel parlare* ("to sound good") or know how to perform a skill—such as embroidery or dance—that *fa figura*. This performance aspect can veer slightly away from the truth, so that sometimes very subtle deception is implied. For example, a woman can be told to "*lasciati il cappello se vuoi far figura*" ("leave your hat on if you want to *far figura*") when her hair is unattractive that day. The *Grande Dizionario Hazon Garzanti: Inglese-Italiano, Italiano-Inglese*, the first edition of which was published in Milan in 1961, includes *fare la figura dello sciocco* (1372) to mean "to play the part of a fool" or "to act the fool."[6]

Minor ramifications to *fare [bella] figura* exist as well. In *Il Nuovo Vocabulario della Lingua Italiana*, published in Florence in 1897, the adverbial phrase *di figura* (literally "of figure") is defined as "*di cosa che ha bella apparenza, a cui non sempre corrisponde l'intrinseco*" ("about something which has a beautiful appearance, whose appearance does not always correspond to the reality of it") (725). The example is "*mobilie di figura, ma costano poco*" which means "furniture *di figura* but which is inexpensive" (725). The word *figura* itself can also refer to a geometric figure, a personnage, a rhetorical figure, a dance position, and the exterior of something, especially the human body. In these ways it is not unlike the English word "figure" to which it also refers in the sense of, literally, a physically "beautiful figure."

Interestingly, if no adjective is used for *figura, bella* is intended. For example, to simply *far figura* means to look good. Sometimes, though, the negative tone of an utterance can substitute for an adjective in carrying the message of *brutta*. *Che figura che ho fatto!* ("What a figure I made!") said in a tone of dismay implies a catastrophe.

Both *figura*, from the Latin *figura*, and *far figura* have a long tradition in written Italian. *Il Vocabulario degli accademici della crusca*, a dictionary published in Florence in 1612 by a group founded in 1583 and comparable to l'academie française, includes literary references to the term which go at least as far back as the 1500s. One example refers to the term in its rhetorical sense: "*la figura é quasi un abito del quale il parlare si veste e s'adorna*" ("figure is almost a suit with which speaking dresses and adorns itself") (1123). From Manzoni's *I Promessi Sposi*, written in the middle 1800s, comes "*Per quanto noi desideriamo di far fare buona figura al nostro povero montanaro . . .*" ("Inasmuch as we want our poor mountain boy to make 'buona figura' . . ."; ["*buona* or "good" is an unusual replacement for "*bella*"]).

Il Nuovo Vocabolario della Lingua Italiana, also published in Florence in 1897, gives the following examples of meaning:

É un uomo che fa figura nelle conversazioni.
(He's a man who makes *figura* in conversations.)

Nel Parlamento ci fa figura.
(He or she makes *figura* in Parliament.)

Cosí non si fa figura.
(This isn't the way to make *figura*.)

É un bravo ragazzo, ma nelle scuole non ci fece mai figura.
(He's a good boy but in school he never made *figura*.)

Quella donna ai suoi tempi faceva figura.
(In her heydey that woman used to make *figura*.) (124)

Experts' opinions vary on precise meaning of the term *bella figura*, although all agree on the importance of its public quality.

Margherita Pieracci Harwell, an Italian native who is an associate professor of Italian at the University of Illinois at Chicago, agrees that *fare figura* is a central metaphor—if not THE central metaphor—to Italian life. "*Figurare vuol dire farsi notare,*" says Harwell. "*La figura é sempre legata all'apparenza. Se uno stesse rinchiuso in una stanza non conterebbe nulla.*" ("To figure means to make oneself be noticed. *Figura* is always linked to appearance. If one were to remain closed up in a room *figura* would not count at all.") She stresses the public quality of *figura*: what difference would appearance make if there were no audience to appreciate it?

Another native informant, Marisa Bonaccorsi, sees *figura* as a code of conduct: "*Bella figura* is to behave in appropriate ways—it shows you're not wanting. You go out of your way so people won't criticize you." Native Francesco Nardini agrees that *bella figura* courts societal approval for both men and women. "*Bella figura* has no gender," he says; "it has social class more than gender. It is like a Sunday dress almost, something you put on to masquerade what you actually are; you try to be part of the group that already has the social status that you are looking for."

Anthropologist Sydel Silverman links the concept with *civiltá*, a sense of civility which she views as one of the main themes of the urban traditions of Central Italy. She comments:

> The concern with one's *bella figura*, or "good face," is ever-present as a quite self-conscious guide to behavior. The concept is a measure of personal integrity, but it has little to do with one's essence, character, intention, or other inner condition; rather it centers upon public appearances. To acquire and preserve *bella figura* requires

being impeccable before the eyes of others. Physically, one must be as immaculate and elegant as possible; if not at all times, given the necessities of work, then at least when engaging in social interaction after work. One must always present a pleasant face to the world, regardless of the negative emotions that may simmer behind it. One must carefully observe the formalities already described; even an unintentional violation will cause a person to bemoan [of himself], "*Ho fatto brutta figura!*" One must show oneself to be knowledgeable of the proper order of rights and obligations in social relations. (A butcher's wife once lamented to me about the *brutta figura* she had made for erring in a judgment of two of her customers' relative social rank and awarding the last available pork chop to the wrong one.) (*Three Bells of Civilization* 40)

According to Harwell, *bella figura* is both class and age related. While it has to do with the image that one wants to present, Harwell sees this image as differentiated according to gender. She thinks that for men *bella figura* has to do with power and with sex—if a woman turns a man down, he will *fare brutta figura*. She thinks that for a woman the issue has to do with a more extensive series of issues: gentility, grace, thinking about others. She said, "*Per la donna la bella figura ha tante piccole faccette. É il desiderio di essere ammirate esteso in tanti campi.*" ("For the woman *bella figura* has many small facets. It is the desire to be admired extended to many different fields.")

An example from contemporary Italy may prove helpful in understanding these small facets. Here the current mores say that wedding gifts must be expensive in order to *fare bella figura*. As in the U.S., there exists a "*lista delle nozze*" ("bridal registry") in Italy, and guests have a sense of how much to spend in order to do the right thing. "*Per i regali di nozze pagano delle cifre enormi—entra la bella figura perché se io faccio un regalo da 50,000 e mio fratello lo fa di 500,000 poi faccio brutta figura,*" specifies Harwell. ("For wedding gifts they spend enormous sums—*bella figura* enters in because, if I give a 50,000 lire gift and my brother gives 500,000, I make an

ugly figure.") Invited to the wedding of the daughter of a friend of
hers, Harwell asked the mother what she could buy for a wedding
present. The mother said that she could buy her daughter "*mutandine*" ("panties"), to Harwell's mind a strangely inexpensive and
private gift. It turned out that these *mutandine* were hand-
embroidered silk panties which cost 180,000 lire each, in today's
money, about $150. The girl's close friends were in fact going out
and buying them for her so she would have a set of six.

Harwell's explanation for this peculiar gift request—which
seemed at first to challenge her evaluation of the family as *senza
pretese* ("without pretensions")—concentrated on the point of display. Obviously, the girl was not going to run around in her
panties. But she still could *fare bella figura* because gifts get shown
to family and to friends. So the *mutandine* did more than just satisfy
the Italian taste for beauty; they also created the appropriate effect
on others when being shown off as a lovely wedding gift. "*Una
parte di questo lusso é legato al fatto che si possono fare vedere. La bella
figura é qualchecosa che porta ammirazione*," says Harwell. ("Part of
this extravagance is linked to the fact that they [the gifts] can be
shown. *Bella figura* is something which engenders admiration.")[7]

Harwell spoke at length about how the manifestation of *bella
figura* has changed in contemporary Italy. For example, forty years
ago women would never have used "*parolaccie*" ("bad words"—
perhaps we would say "swear words" or "coarse language") for
fear of being judged unrefined themselves. Now relatives report to
her that some women say, "*Non m'importa una sega*" ("I don't give
a shit") along with the men.

As a case in point, Harwell related an instance of a store clerk
who, while waiting on her in refined fashion, was simultaneously
talking on the phone. The clerk was reporting to a friend about her
participation in a protest against Italy's old-fashioned universities.
Unabashed, she mentioned that the sign she carried had said, "*Non
mi rompere la vagina*." ("Don't bust my vagina" is a sort of female
rendition of "Don't bust my balls" or "*Non mi rompere i coglioni*.")
Apparently, the clerk considered this language not at odds with
waiting on customers. She was not attacking Harwell, but lambast-
ing a university system that she considered anti-female. The point,

however, is her use of the language at all. Harwell said that some years ago such *parolaccie* would never have been used (and certainly not publicly) by a young woman in front of an older woman in a public setting. It would have meant untold *brutta figura*.

However, upon further reflection, Harwell said, "*Le cose sono cambiate ma non sono cambiate tanto. É eterno proprio.*" ("Things have changed but they haven't changed a lot. It's really eternal.") She gave as proof another story about Filomena, the same woman alleged to have said, "*Non m'importa una sega.*"

It is necessary to understand the Italian class system of fifty years ago to see what Harwell means. Filomena, in her seventies, is the cousin of the man who used to be the *contadino* ("one from the country" or "peasant" or "farmer," here used in the sense of "caretaker of the land") for the property which Harwell's family owned. She herself had been the *donna di servizio* ("nursemaid") in charge of the nine year old Harwell. Now this former "*donna di servizio-contadina*" lives happily as a retired housewife in a lovely condominium with her married daughter. They are "*chiaramente arricchiti*" ("clearly grown rich").

"*Contadino*" means "farmer," literally, but it is often used to mean "rustic" or "peasant" in a sense which is deprecatory—almost like "redneck" in English. According to Silverman, the level of "*civiltá*" ("civility") in Colleverde, a hilltop village in the province of Perugia not dissimilar from Harwell's own Tuscan village, is the most important indicator of prestige stratification. Among other qualities, this concept includes "a number of specifically urban patterns: fashionable clothing, nonrustic habitation, refined manners, nondialectal speech, participation in the cafe-and-piazza social life, and access (direct or indirect) to larger centers" ("An Ethnographic Approach" 912). A *contadino*, presumably, would have few of these prestige qualities; even an ex-*contadino* who has taken on village "ways" (by moving from the country or changing his *mezzadro* work status) is still "indelibly identified" (911) as in the lower prestige category.

In the elevator of the condominium one day, Filomena pointed out a neighbor with hostility, "*Vede quella donna lí? É una grande scema perché sa che cosa mi ha detto? 'Ma tu eri una contadina?*

Perché si vede' . . . Pensi che ignorante!" ("Do you see that woman? She's a big dope because do you know what she said to me? 'But were you a *contadina*? Because you can see [that you were].' Just think how ignorant!")

According to Harwell, Filomena was obviously offended by the remark. However, her sense of the remark as insult had nothing to do with concealment, since Harwell knew her origins. After all, she had worked for Harwell's family. Also, according to Harwell, there is nothing the matter in today's Italy with looking like a "*contadina*." Harwell says, "*Perché lei si offende? Non dovrebbe. Cinquanta anni fa uno nascondeva la sua condizione sociale. Ma in questi ultimi anni c'é stata tutta una campagna per valorizzare il popolo versus la piccola borghesia. L'implicazione é che se uno non é nato principe allora meglio che sia nato contadino.*" ("Why is she offended? She shouldn't be. Fifty years ago one hid one's social condition. But in these last years there's been a big campaign [she means by the Communist Party] ennobling the advantages of the masses versus the bourgeoisie. The implication is that if you aren't born a prince, then it's better to be born a peasant.")

But Filomena had apparently maintained intact the notion of *bella figura* unchanged from years ago. To BE a "*contadina*" is one thing, but to look like one is too close to the negative meaning of the word for comfort. Even though her language made her appear "*più evoluta, non si era evoluta nel modo di pensare*" ("more evolved, she hadn't evolved in her way of thinking"). For, as Harwell mentioned with some irony, "*Se le avesse detto 'sembra una maestra' non si sarebbe offesa.*" ("If they had told her, 'you look like an [elementary school] teacher' she wouldn't have been offended.") This example shows the extraordinary importance of non-*contadina* appearance to the issue of *bella figura*.

Giovanna Del Negro concurs. In a dissertation which studies the *passeggiata* or "promenade," the ritual stroll up and down the piazza in the hour before dinner, she says:

> In Sasso the cultural desire to *fare bella figura* is collectively reenacted everytime Sassani perform their ritual *vasche*

> (laps) down the main thoroughfare. . . . [Here] the con-
> summate art of display is given full reign. With its empha-
> sis on appearance, *bella figura* is largely measured in terms
> of demeanor and presentational style. . . . The most tal-
> ented performers . . . usually possess what the Italians call
> *disinvoltura* (ease of manners) . . . , spontaneous and above
> all free from affectation. (*"Our Little Paris": Gender, Popu-*
> *lar Culture and the Promenade in Central Italy* 52–55)

This notion of self as a social presentation for the consumption of
others is widespread in the Mediterranean world. It is linked to
the reputation which the community awards to its members. According to Pitkin, it represents "a kind of displacement of the interior self to the exterior where it becomes constructed as social
fact. One is, for purposes of social discourse, what one is perceived
to be" (98). Of course, this community of the *passeggiata* needs to
be urban in orientation—piazza-like—rather than rural in order to
provide the necessary audience to judge the *figura*. Since actors
and audience are forever changing roles, the system continues to
perpetuate itself for, according to Del Negro, "everywhere people
are surrounded by mirrors" (4).

The concept of "honor and shame and the values of Mediterranean society" (Peristiany, Pitt-Rivers, among others) is useful in
fixing a paradigm in which to place this development of a constructed social self as *figura*.[8] In his vision of the Mediterranean as a
geographical whole, that is, as a former Roman colony consisting
of Spain, France, Italy, Greece, and northern Africa—a concept he
and other anthropologists first discussed in 1959 at Burg Warten-
stein—Peristiany sets up honor and shame as a binary opposition
in which

> Honour and shame are the constant preoccupation of in-
> dividuals in small scale, exclusive societies where face-to-
> face personal, as opposed to anonymous, relations are of
> paramount importance and where the social personality of
> the actor is as significant as his office. (11)

The functioning of this paradigm depends, to some extent, upon honor being what Foster describes as a "limited good"; that is, actors must forever court public opinion—of which there is a finite amount—in order to be worthy of it.

Julio Caro Baroja associates the Spanish *honor* (in Italian, *onore*) with a medieval development arising from the *honos, honoris* of classical Latin meaning "ideas of respect, esteem and prestige . . . and . . . rewards, ornaments and clothes which elevate their bearer above the rest of the community" (82–83). He links the Spanish *verguenza* ("shame"; in Italian, *vergogna*) with the Latin *verecundia*, defined as "not only chastity and modesty . . . but also as respect for parents and elders . . . and as humility, reserve and respect for the laws and their representatives" (87). Then, in a series of complicated historical changes, he explains how these two concepts, both all-pervasive in the circum-Mediterranean, come to depend upon specific gender roles, especially upon notions of female chastity.

Clearly, this is a value system which favors men. That is, honor goes to the man who keeps his women chaste and shame to the man whose women are unchaste. A woman's honor lies solely in guarding her "shame," a particular demureness protecting her chastity, while a man's honor can also be won through other exploits with his social equals (other men). Therefore, shame can be both male and female while honor is exclusively male.

In 1987, David Gilmore set about to "reexamine fundamental assumptions about Mediterranean unity made on the basis of the original honor/shame model" (2). He edited *Honor and Shame and the Unity of the Mediterranean*, acknowledging once again these specifically Mediterranean traits. But he added the crucial point that manifestations of honor and shame vary from country to country. For example, Michael Herzfeld proposes hospitality in place of honor, as he analyzes his ethnographic data from Greece. Other authors in this volume also extend Peristiany's original concepts. Stanley Brandes describes Spanish settings in which the word *honor* is rarely employed while *verguenza* (shame) appears frequently as a quality for both men and women. Michael Marcus describes Moroccan honor among rural strongmen of the past as a facet of cooperation, rather than competition, as was previously thought. These researchers extend Mediterranean anthropology to include "a culturally, politically, and historically localized discourse" (Herzfeld 88).

While emphasizing the critical importance of gender perceptions and gender roles, Gilmore also questions what he calls the "sexual-contest perception" (5) as a distortion of contemporary Mediterranean values. To view women's chastity as overarchingly important in all of Italy, for example, is an oversimplification, according to Gilmore. In fact, Maureen Giovannini—whose research in Sicily shows female chastity codes as still important there (65)—reiterates Silverman's account, which proves the opposite to be true elsewhere.

In 1968 Silverman stated:

> In a sense, the values related to sex have some basis in the agricultural system. Family honor in Southern Italy, as in other Mediterranean areas, is largely vested in the virginity of the girls. Masculinity is asserted (sometimes violently) by the protection of one's own virgins, the vindication of one's violated girls, and the conquest of other families' virgins. *In Central Italy, these themes of virginity and the contest over it are much softened. Girls have considerable freedom of movement, loss of virginity is not taken seriously, violence is almost unheard of, and the whole subject is injected with humor.* ("Agricultural Organization" 16; emphasis mine)

Therefore, setting aside the absolutist concern with female chastity, and allowing for country-by-country differences, particularity in the naming of honor and shame, this paradigm would seem to work in Italy. Specifically, it makes sense that the concepts of honor and shame create external constraints or boundaries in a society where personhood is paraded in the piazza—rather than located in the inner self and bounded by guilt.

Peter Burke, a cultural historian, re-iterates this anthropological concept when he speaks of "three Europes: north-western, southern, and eastern. Thus, Southern Europe, Mediterranean Europe, was Romance-speaking, Catholic . . . with an outdoor culture . . . and a value-system laying great stress on honour and shame" (*Popular Culture* 57).

In Italy, specifically, *figura* can be thought of as encompassing both honor and shame. That is, *bella figura* represents "honor" (a word in most Italian contexts seldom mentioned) and *brutta figura* "shame" or *vergogna* (a word more frequently mentioned). Shame or *brutta figura* is, above all, visual and public—it requires an audience. "In the psychic mechanism of shaming, it is the 'eye' of the community and the related sense of paranoic observation that are assimilated to worldview and to personality" (Gilmore 101). Thus, the absorption with making a *bella figura*. Gender identification is linked in the way that men and women make *bella figura*— that is, the roles are acted out in distinct, sometimes contrasting fashion—but both sexes have equal access to the benefits of performing well. In its revisionary view, this is not a particularly sexist system.

It is, however, one which remains difficult to understand for those who have internalized the notion of self as an interior mechanism restrained by guilt. Many Americans, regardless of their specific ethnicities, have learned to valorize the "idealization of the rural in English thought and the mythification of nature in German consciousness" (Pitkin 99). These landscapes are the opposite of the "urbanscape" which Pitkin links to the making of a *bella figura*. Of necessity, someone who speaks of the "inner self" as found in communing with nature—the English romantics, for example, gave rise to what Burke calls a "culture of sincerity" (*Fortunes* 108)—tends to see the putting on of a *figura* as a kind of deception. While there is, according to Del Negro, "always some level of artifice and impression management involved" (personal e-mail correspondence), to see *figura* as exclusively (or even primarily) put-on is to miss the point.

Many American writers do. Casillo, for example, speaks of Jake La Motta in the film *Raging Bull* as attempting to claim for himself

that violence and invulnerability that pagan religions as-
cribe to the gods. Thus he would achieve the ultimate
bella figura—godlike status in the eyes of a simultaneously
idolatrous and envious crowd for which all-powerful violence is the unacknowledged sign of divinity. (391)

But *bella figura* is not a sometime thing—not a showing off which
is controlled only by certain circumstances. Rather, it is a deeper,
more constant construction performed all the time, mostly as a
matter of course. This is not to say that Jake La Motta was not
claiming for himself "the ultimate *bella figura*"—he probably was;
but, in so doing, he was not restricting the meaning of it to violent
spectacle. His choice of violent performance—and the crowd's
adulation of it—are ethical issues separate from his performance of
bella figura.

Another misunderstanding occurs in Fred Gardaphe's analysis
of *The Godfather*.

In the Don's speech to the heads of the other crime families after the murder of Sonny, he attempts to make peace
through an appeal to the American Dream, but the whole
speech is an example of *bella figura*, a public posturing designed to shield his true plans and to present the illusion
that he is willing to assimilate to the American ways of
doing illegal business. (91)

But the performance of *bella figura* does not get turned on and off,
in almost schizophrenic fashion, by the Italian performing it. This
is not to say that the Don's speech could not have been duplici-
tous, a "public posturing designed to shield his true plans"—it
certainly could have been. But the *bella* (or *brutta*) *figura* of it is a
separate issue. If the Don's intention had been to express honest
thinking and feeling, his rhythmical language, poetic use of
metaphor, and parallel constructions would have been just as good
an example of *bella figura*. In fact, his creation of ethos—a sort of
us-*v.*-them mentality implicit in "None of us here want to see our

children follow in our footsteps" (91)—is quintessential *bella figura*. Veracity, or the lack thereof, has nothing to do with anything in this case.

Helen Barolini, American-born author of *Umbertina*, also misunderstands this notion of facade: "I lived a long while in Italy and came to associate it with a kind of cover-up—where there was little or no substance, style (*bella figura*) could make the effect" (personal correspondence).

What all of these interpretations share is a peculiarly American naiveté which sees *figura* as somehow separate from the true self, the pristine, unadorned self. They fail to comprehend the very subtle, all-encompassing, and public ways in which the expression of Italian identity is imbricated in creating *bella figura*. Thus, those who ask, "Where is the real person behind the *bella figura*?" fail to understand the point: *bella figura* is a social construction of identity that depends upon public performance for its reification. In its "interaction between personal aspiration and assessment by others" (Pitkin 98), it becomes part of the real person's creation and presentation of self. To oversimplify, the "real person" is *in* the *bella figura*.

A mention of the etymological history of the word "performance" is in order here, for one American difficulty in misunderstanding *figura* may lie in the way in which these two concepts are linked. While *The Oxford English Dictionary* clearly defines "performance" as "the action of performing a ceremony, play, part in a play, piece of music, etc., formal or set execution" (543), it also lists many other meanings for the word. Among them are "the carrying out of a duty" and "the execution of anything undertaken"; other definitions denote psychological and/or linguistic meanings. The root word "perform" comes from Middle English adapted from the Old French *par— perfourmer —furmer —former—* meaning either "to carry through in due form" or "to accomplish entirely." Thus, in general, "performance" implies a doing of something undertaken as a task.

In all eleven definitions from *The Oxford English Dictionary*, the word "performance" has only one slightly negative meaning: a twentieth century definition of "display of temperament, anger or exaggerated behavior, a fuss or 'scene' " (544). The verb "perform" also has no negative meanings except for its use in recent Australian slang: "to display extreme anger or bad temper; to swear loudly; to make a great fuss" (544). Why then the American tendency to limit the meaning of the word to its stage concept? Why associate it with behavior which covers up or is somehow lacking in veracity? This limitation seems of recent date.

Some Historical Notions

An impressionistic and cursory note on Italian history is in order here. Romano claims that thirty centuries of Italian identity begin with the Romans who provide "*Un modello costituito dal diritto, dalla lingua, da un certo senso della vita di relazione (teatri, terme, arene . . .)*" (5). ("A model constituted by law, language, and *a certain sense of social life [theatres, baths, arenas . . .]*"; [emphasis mine]). If we construe this phrase to mean an understanding of human relations as public and performed, then Roman influence on Italian identity can be linked to *bella figura*.

The importance of ceremony can also be traced to the Middle Ages. Speaking of feudalism Romano says:

L'aspetto formale é presente anche nell'atto di vassallaggio: il vassus pone le mani in quelle del signore, manifestando in tal modo il suo totale darsi a quest'ultimo, il quale, a sua volta, con poche parole accetta l'offerta del vassus. Intervengono dunque, parole e gesti e, molto probabilmente, sono piú i secondi che le prime, ad avere peso e senso. (40)

[The formal aspect is present even in the act of vassallage: the vassal puts his hands into the lord's, thus demonstrating his total giving of himself to the latter, who, in his turn, accepts with few words the offer of the vassal. Therefore, both words and gestures occur, and, *very probably, the gestures have more weight and meaning than the words.*] (Emphasis mine)

This investiture can also be linked to *bella figura* in the sense that real benefits—loyalty to the lord, on the one hand, and use of the land by the vassal, on the other—occur through a symbolic act in which the public performance of the gestures carries the meaning.

Harwell traces *bella figura* in particular to Castiglione's *The Book of the Courtier*, the first draft of which was composed in 1508, during the height of the Renaissance. The Renaissance rendered Italians famous for their art, their food, their decorating, their design, their artisanship, their music, their grace, a reputation which they retain today. It is interesting to note that all these elements depend upon a visual performance for their effect.[9]

Italians seem to have always been very good at spectacle. Burke speaks of Italy as

> the best evidence for improvised drama in the *commedia dell'arte* . . . often known during this time as *commedia al-l'improviso*. Whether Italians extemporised more readily than other performers or whether their performances have simply been recorded more carefully, it is difficult to say. (*Popular Culture* 143)

Either way, attention to *figura* seems paramount, for the recording itself is a testimony to the importance of spectacle.

In fact, Jacob Burckhardt describes a "national passion for external display" (274) as a singular characteristic of Italian Renaissance during which the "chief points of superiority in the Italian festivals" are described as "the capacity to invent a given mask, and to act the part with dramatic propriety" (301). He describes in great detail the "pomp and brilliancy" (300) of the secular *Trionfi* ("triumphs") modeled on the processions of the Roman Imperator. No efforts were spared: in Milan, the great Leonardo directed pantomimes! In Venice festival processions, replete with allegorical figures and elaborate masks, moved on water.

The strong historic sense of the Italians allowed them to group and compose characters and scenes effectively; the public was a competent critic of this piazza artistry, having seen it all their lives. This creation of literary, political, spiritual, and historical performances with a "view to splendid and striking scenic effects" (307) emphasizes the idea of *figura* and also makes it available on a regular basis. Mystery plays, feast-day processions, great court festivals, brilliant pantomimes, Carnival—some of which continue today— were a continuance of Italian national life as performance. Says Burckhardt, "The Italian festivals in their best form mark a point of transition from real life into the world of art" (2).

Another example of the continuing importance of historical tradition is provided by the medieval cathedral found in Barga, a nucleated center of 5,000 in the province of Lucca. A plaque is mounted on this Duomo with the words of adopted citizen, romantic poet Giovanni Pascoli. Written in the late 1800s, the inscription says:

> Al tempo dei tempi, avanti il Mille, i Barghigiani campavano rosicchiando castagne, e fecero il Duomo. Dicevano: "in casa mia ch'io salti anche da un travicello all'altro; benedetta libertá." Ma il Duomo ha da essere grande, col piú bel pulpito di marmo che si possa vedere e col piú forte dei Santi. Dicevano: "Piccolo il mio, Grande il nostro."

> [Once upon a time, before the year 1000, people from Barga got by by gnawing on chestnuts, and they built the Duomo. They would say, "In my house let me even jump from beam to beam; who cares!" But the Duomo must be large, with the most beautiful marble pulpit that anyone has ever seen; and with the holiest of Saints. They would say: "Let mine be little, but ours should be big."]

Pascoli's words blend the real-life efforts of the anonymous stone masons and carvers and painters and sculptors who built the Duomo with the world of art to which the building now belongs. The "transition" which he provides, this linking of the past with the present, depends upon an understanding of the *figura* which the participants wished to create. It is fascinating to see this viewpoint, separated by nine centuries, evidence itself with the same singularity of intent! Additional credence to the *bella figura* lies in the fact that the plaque was erected to celebrate the reconstruction of the Duomo during the Fascist Era.

Castiglione, who himself served in the Court of the Duke of Urbino from 1504 to 1508, intends to describe

> the trade and maner of courtiers, which is most convenient for a gentleman that liveth in the Court of Princes, by the which he may have the knowledge how to serve them perfitely in every reasonable matter, and obtaine thereby favour of them, and praise of other men. (15)

Evoking a "tradition of behavior to which Aristotle, Cicero, rules for monks, and courtesy books for knights and ladies all made contributions" (Burke, *Fortunes* 153), this decidedly upper-class experience becomes especially important to the practice of good manners throughout Western Europe. Of particular importance is the way in which the perfect Italian chooses understated elegance:

> Therefore will I have our Courtier to descend many times to more easie and pleasant exercises . . . .but let him laugh, dally, jest, and daunce, yet in such wise that he may alwaies declare him selfe to be wittie and discreete, and every thing that hee doth or speaketh, let him doe it with a grace. . . .
> *Therefore that may bee saide to be a verie arte, that appeareth not to be arte, neither ought a man to put more diligence in any thing than in covering it: for in case it be open, it looseth credite cleane and maketh a man litle set by.* (Castiglione 49, 53; emphasis mine)

In short, Castiglione heralds here the kind of artful grace which appears artless; it is a further ramification of the connection between appearance and *bella figura*. Castiglione calls this quality *sprezzatura*, (mistranslated by Hoby as "reckelesness"). The term implies a studied carelessness, a nonchalant display which conceals the efforts expended to acquire it.

Apparently coined by Castiglione himself, *sprezzatura* is a noun which means "*maniera negletta e disinvolta di fare, dire e simile propria, di chi é molto sicuro di sé*" ("careless and nonchalant manner of doing, saying, and similar activities, of one who is very sure of himself") (*Il Nuovo Zingarelli* 1883). It is a derivative of the verb *sprezzare*, an alternate of *disprezzare* (to disdain), which means *non curare* (to not pay attention to) from the Vulgar Latin *expretiare* consisting of *pretium* (esteem) and *ex* (not). Therefore, the implication is that in order to achieve *sprezzatura*, one must act in a manner which accords little (ostensible) attention to one's actions. Cox adds, "Castiglione's term . . . has an added inflection of aristocratic contempt for any appearance of effort or strain" (380). Bonora says, "*É il contrario dell'affettazione e dote essenziale del cortigiano che senza di essa non potrá raggiungere la 'grazia'*" (It is the opposite of affectation and an essential quality of the courtier who, without it, cannot achieve 'grace'") (62).

In fact, "*grazia*" is mentioned over and over in *Il Cortigiano*, especially in Books 1 and 2 where the qualities of the perfect courtier are extensively described. He is to be a graceful physical specimen: not too small nor too large, a horseman able to use weapons gracefully and to wrestle. He should also speak eloquently, he should love "letters" and music and art, dance well, and wear sober, restrained clothes, especially black or dark colors. In short, he should be as elegant and attractive as he is competent and discreet.

Interestingly, the Italian definitions for *grazia* are quite different from the English ones. *Il Nuovo Zingarelli* reports the first two as:

1. *Sensazione di piacere che destano le cose per la loro naturalezza, semplicitá, delicatezza, armonia* (Sensation of pleasure which is awakened by virtue of the naturalness, simplicity, delicacy, and harmony of things)
2. *Amabilitá, gentilezza nei rapporti con gli altri: . . . misurata gentilezza negli atti esteriori* (Amiability, courtesy in relations with others . . . measured politeness in outward acts). (847)

Notice the emphasis upon the performance aspects here: in the first definition, the *grazia* arises from its ability to arouse pleasure-able feelings in (one supposes) the onlooker, implying an overt act; in the second, both the "relations with others" and "outward acts" require behavior performed in front of an audience.

In English, on the other hand, "grace" is defined as

1. beauty or charm of form, composition, movement, or expression; elegance with appropriate dignity
2. an attractive quality, feature, manner, etc.
3. a sense of what is right and proper; decency. (*Webster's* 790)

Only in the twelfth definition for the noun form of "grace" is there any mention of performability, and then that mention is a mocking one: "affectation of elegance; assumption of refinement; as, he laughed at her airs and *graces*" (790).

Above all, as Cesare Gonzaga is told when he asks how the courtier should gain this "*grazia,*" which is not natural to every-one—the man should be free from "*affettazione*" (affectation) de-fined as "*mancanza di naturalezza*" (lack of naturalness) (Zingarelli 38). Notice the link between this use of "*naturalezza*" and its use in the first definition of "*grazia.*" So both terms—lack of affecta-tion and grace—hinge upon a naturalness of behavior and look observable as *sprezzatura.*

Such behavior does not have to *be* natural, however; it must simply look like it is—what Burke calls the "paradox of sprez-zatura" (*Fortunes* 154). Castiglione says:

And in every thing that he hath to do or to speake, if it be possible, lette him come *alwaies provided and thinke on it beefore hande,* showying notwithstanding, the whole to bee done ex tempore, and at the first sight. (146; emphasis mine)

Such staging is not to be considered "deceit," but rather "an orna-ment that accompanyeth the thinge he doeth" (148), much like the setting the goldsmith makes to enhance a precious jewel. So, too, the courtier should "where he knoweth those prayses that are geven him to be true: let hym not so openly consent to them, nor confirme them so without resistance, but rather with modesty (in a manner) denye them cleane" (81). Burckhardt's interpretation supports this gentlemanly performance—of modesty and pretended extemporaneousness—for he sees the courtier as "the ideal man of society . . . regarded by the civilization of that age as its choicest flower; the court existed for him rather than he for the court" (287).

Castiglione, of course, is only one example of Italy's role in leading Western Europe to humanism. But in what Bull calls the "most representative book of the Renaissance" (12), it is important to note that Castiglione stresses balance in the *bella figura* performance of his gentleman. This courtier should "doe whatsoever other men doe" but "with a grace" (49) that distinguishes him. Burke refers to this as an illustration of "social life as a work of art" (*Fortunes* 138). Natalino Sapegno, whose treatise *Disegno Storico della Letteratura Italiana* ("*Historic Overview of Italian Literature*") was studied by Italian secondary school students for generations, states:

> Nell'immagine del cortigiano si concreta la parte piú alta dello spirito del Rinascimento: l'ideale dell'uomo che ha conquistato la piena consapevolezza delle cose e il perfetto dominio di se stesso, che ha ordinato la propria vita secondo una legge di mirabile equilibrio, in un'armoniosa concordia delle facoltá fisiche e delle spirituali, delle esigenze individuali e sociali, dell'uomo e della natura. . . . Letterariamente il Cortegiano é uno dei libri piú belli del Cinquecento, in quanto realizza pur nello stile quell'idea di compostezza luminosa e pacata, quella eleganza chiara e senza affettazione, che era la norma fondamentale della cortesia. (245)

> [In the image of the courtier the highest spirit of the Renaissance is made concrete: the ideal of the man who has conquered full knowledge of things and perfect

control over himself, who has ordered his own life with admirable equilibrium, in a harmonious balance between physical and spiritual faculties, between individual and social needs, between man and nature. . . . In literature the *Cortegiano* is one of the most beautiful books of the *Cinquecento*, inasmuch as even its style itself realizes that idea of serene and luminous dignity, of clear and unaffected elegance, which was the fundamental norm of courtesy.]

Such a concept of balance seems to reflect the attention that all of European Humanism gave to society: it created a renewed interest in the classics at the same time that it paid attention to the individual, thus causing a rediscovery of autonomous human values, especially artistic ones. Cox says, "It is a premise—or a promise—of *The Courtier* that the behavioural ethos it elaborates will provide a formula for social success in contexts far removed from the court of Urbino in 1507" (xxiii). Perhaps, therefore, a case can be made for the notion of *bella figura* as the perfect expression of the Italian Renaissance humanist.

Two other periods are worthy of mention in chronicling the historical evidence of *bella figura*; both of them flower in Rome. One is the Baroque in Italian art, from 1550 to about 1750, described by Salvatorelli as a style that "*dette uno straordinario sviluppo alla decorazione facendola scopo a se stessa*" (353) ("developed decoration to an extraordinary extent making it its own reason for existence"). Barzini contends that the virtuosismo of this period was an attempt by the Italians

> to find compensation for the insecurity, emptiness, disarray, impotence and despair of their national life, to forget their humiliation and shame, to forget their collective guilt. It was a frenzied search for consolation and revenge against the crude and overbearing foreign devils. (309)

The "devils" referred to are the Spanish, who held dominion over Italy for several centuries. Although Barzini's analysis may appear overly simplified and sentimental, the Baroque is usually looked upon as quintessential decoration—or *bella figura*—and Italy is usually looked upon as the quintessential Baroque.

The second period is Fascism, an era in which political expediency appropriates for itself the concepts of *bella figura*. Salvatorelli calls it

> una grandiosa politica di lavori pubblici (non senza eccessi e ostentazione). . . . [A] Roma vennero eseguiti scavi archeologici imponenti e con la liberazione dei fori imperiali si creó la 'via dell'Impero', ma si alteró anche malamente, con distruzioni e costruzioni arbitrarie, la fisionomia della citta. (500–01)

> [a grandiose politics of public works (not without excess and ostentation) . . . [I]n Rome imposing archeological excavations were executed and with the liberation of imperial forums [, the fascist regime] created 'The Imperial Way', but it also badly altered the face of the city through senseless razing and ugly constructions]

Fascism's early success, according to Andreucci, is dependent in part upon Mussolini's "exploitation of Italy's imperial Roman heritage in the symbols and settings of his regime" (230); much is made during this era of uniforms and parades, posters and slogans, orations and propaganda—all designed to dazzle. Italy's alliance with Nazi Germany (coupled with an unpopular anti-semitic stance) leads, however, to a lessening of fascist popularity. Finally, the extensive course of her military operations in World War II creates total Italian rejection of the fascist regime. To continue the metaphor to its extreme, Mussolini's scapegoating can be viewed as a punishment for the dictator who becomes, in the eyes of the world, the quintessential *brutta figura*.

While I am not a historian and make no claim for systematic, scholarly, and detailed analysis of the above events, I think it is significant that the *zeitgeist* of entirely different political and economic eras can be felt in comments on both *bella* and *brutta figura*. Lakoff and Johnson claim that

Metaphors may create realities for us, especially social realities. A metaphor may thus be a guide for future action.
Such actions will, of course, fit the metaphor. This will,
in turn, reinforce the power of the metaphor to make
experience coherent. In this sense metaphors can be self-
fulfilling prophecies. (156)

This is my point: expectations about the importance of *bella
figura*—and the avoidance of *brutta figura*—play themselves out
constantly within Italian constructions of history.

It is not necessary, however, to discuss important historical
data in order to understand *bella figura*, for the notion encompasses
a sense of theatricality and performance within ordinary activities
as well. It is constitutive of an Italian's worldview—when one
moves from role to role, one does not lose "essence," so to speak;
one simply shifts functions. In this way, *bella figura* can be likened
to the concept of performance as explained by sociologist Erving
Goffman. In *The Presentation of Self in Everyday Life,* which he calls
"a sort of handbook . . . from which social life can be studied"
(xi), Goffman defines performance as "all the activity of a given
participant on a given occasion which serves to influence in any
way any of the other participants" (15). Goffman writes:

And when we observe a young American middle-class
girl playing dumb for the benefit of her boy friend, we are
ready to point to items of guile and contrivance in her behavior. But like herself and her boy friend, we accept as
an unperformed fact that this performer *is* a young American middle-class girl. But surely here we neglect the
greater part of the performance. . . . To *be* a given kind of
person . . . is not merely to possess the required attributes,
but also to sustain the standards of conduct and appearance that one's social grouping attaches thereto. The un-
thinking ease with which performers consistently carry off
such standard-maintaining routines does not deny that a
performance has occurred, *merely that the participants have
been aware of it.* (75; emphasis mine)

To think of social life as a theatrical performance implies a kind of learned appropriateness. Goffman tells us that culture has "two common-sense models" for our formulation of behavior: the real, sincere, or honest performance and the false one that fabricators assemble (70). But he deconstructs this notion by showing us that "ordinary social intercourse" is dependent upon "scripts" which are managed even by "unpracticed players" since, after all, "life itself is a dramatically enacted thing" (72). So, even in his (very white, very middle-class) view, we are all playing out our parts. Whether we are taken in by our own acts (and are thus "sincere") or are cynical about them (and thus "false"), they are still "roles."

Goffman uses the term "frame" to identify the principles of organization which govern events and our participation in them. He aims to make plain "the struggle to achieve that apparently effortless sociability" with which face-to-face interaction is concerned (Berger xii). In order to examine experience coherently, he asks, " 'What is it that's going on here?' " (*Frame Analysis* 18); but he is ever aware that the answer may vary according to the different understandings of the people involved. Goffman, in fact, sees performance as "ceremony" when it highlights the common official values of the society in which it occurs. Thus, he would look upon the performance of *bella figura* as "an expressive rejuvenation and reaffirmation of the moral values" of the Italian worldview (*Presentation of Self* 35).

Folklorist Richard Bauman says that performance "sets up . . . an interpretative frame within which the messages being communicated are to be understood" (*Verbal Art* 9). This frame contrasts to the literal. So Bauman, too, has a sense of performance as specific to the community involved, rather as "a frame within a frame" (Farr, informal discussion with author). Of course, Bauman is speaking of linguistic communications; in his approach, performance becomes "*constitutive* of the domain of verbal art" (11). When he refers to "text," he means spoken words, especially narratives.

But Bauman's notion of "text" can be profitably extended by the Goffmanesque lens for, if performance is culturally determined, then "text" too can be culturally determined. In an Italian community—where *bella figura* is a flaunting of self—perhaps "text" can refer to personhood and behavior as well as to "verbal art." Thus, when Bauman talks about "culture-specific ways to key the performance frame" such as "special codes," "appeal to tradition," and "disclaimer of performance," these communicative means for "verbal art" can be looked upon as similar to Castiglione's descriptions of *sprezzatura* in presentation of self.

Bauman says:

> It is part of the essence of performance that it offers to the participants a *special enhancement of experience,* bringing with it a *heightened intensity of communicative interaction* which binds the audience to the performer in a way that is specific to performance as a mode of communication. Through his performance, the performer elicits the participative attention and energy of his audience, and to the extent that they value his performance, they will allow themselves to be caught up in it. (43; emphases mine)

This "special enhancement of experience" which, according to Bauman, "heightens the intensity of communicative interaction" Italians understand culturally as the performance of *bella figura.* Barzini would seem to agree. He explains that in Italy

> the show is as important as, many times more important than, reality. This is perhaps due to the fact that the climate has allowed Italians to live mostly outside their houses, in the streets and *piazze*; they judge men and events less by what they read or learn, and far more by what they see, hear, touch and smell. Or because they are naturally inclined towards arranging a spectacle, acting a character, staging a drama; or because they are more pleased by display than others, to the point that they do not countenance life when it is reduced to unadorned truth. . . . *Whatever the reason, the result is that at all times form and substance are considered one and the same thing. One*

cannot exist without the other. The expression is the thing ex-pressed. (Barzini 89–90; emphasis mine)

I agree with Barzini's analysis. In the sense that theatrics pervade everyday Italian life, and that spontaneous performances can occur within the context of this theatrical everyday life, both Goffman's notion of "self presentation as organizational frame" and Bauman's "performance as interpretative frame" obtain. They can be thought of as the contexts within which *bella figura* is expected, encouraged and constituted.

Thus, when Italians *fare bella figura*, they speak, gesture, act, live with a sense of performance that is second nature. This *sprezzatura* has a deep historical base and a broad moment-by-moment expression. It is reflected in their viewpoint, their language, their art and civic life, the whole of their culture; and it carries over as they encounter other cultures and/or blend into them.

TWO

The Conceptual Framework of this Study and Related Literature on Women's Language

Like all cultural constructs, *bella figura* is inextricably bound to language: this is the principal tenet of my conceptual framework. The study focuses on the communicative competence demonstrated by the ladies of the Collandia Club, where I did participant observation for two-and-one-half years. I mean to assert the absolute primacy of culture, in Geertz's definition as the "webs of significance" we ourselves "have spun" (5), for the interpretation of the meaning of language and language structures (Geertz 5).

Throughout the following chapter I will summarize multiple theoretical contexts important to my research, showing how in each one language and culture always operate together. I will make explicit both the linguistic and the nonlinguistic aspects implicit within communicative competence, thus constructing and then deconstructing its complexities. I will end with a discussion of the links between each part of my conceptual framework and the overarching Italian cultural construction of *fare bella figura* as explicated in Chapter 1.

In the second half of this chapter, I will review the literature on women's language studies throughout which the themes of gender and power appear as constants. My claim will be that in a women's bilingual and bicultural context myriad and subtle communicative strategies, heretofore largely unexplored, exist rather as a matter of course. In addition, understanding how *bella figura* functions as a performance strategy in this context complicates the view of women as powerless users of language. In fact, through *bella figura,* Italian women indirectly assert themselves in order to claim power.

Most students of language regard language as linked to the social context in which it occurs. According to the Sapir-Whorf hypothesis, the structure of the grammar and the vocabulary of a language determine its worldview. This is the strongest possible view of the relationship between language and culture—that is, that thought depends upon the words and cognitive mindsets one has at one's cultural disposition. While most scholars are reluctant to accord Whorf's principle of linguistic relativity its strongest form, many do accept the view that language both reflects and shapes thought; it also guides behavior in some circumstances. Sociolinguist Ralph Fasold states, "[t]o a large degree, the argument has become one of how strong a version of the Whorf hypothesis is credible, rather than whether Whorf was right or wrong" (53). I agree: there is no meaning for language outside of cultural meaning. That is, there is no abstraction of the formal system of language outside its cultural context or use.

When in 1962 Dell Hymes created the ethnography of communication, he understood that ways of speaking can vary substantially from one culture to another. Hymes found shortsighted and limiting both the linguists' fixation on language as an abstract system and the nonchalant absence of fixation displayed by anthropologists, for whom language was simply a means of exploring the important themes of a culture. So he adapted the notion of the speech community, which he defined as a group sharing knowledge of rules for the conduct and interpretation of speech. In acknowledging the importance of social context, Hymes moved the role of language-as-a-system-used-by-real-people-in-real-situations from a subsidiary position to a position of prominence. Of the need for an ethnography of communication Hymes says:

> It is not that linguistics does not have a vital role. Analyzed linguistic materials are indispensable, and the logic of linguistic methodology is an influence in the ethnographic perspective. *It is rather that it is not linguistics, but ethnography, not language, but communication, which must provide the frame of reference within which the place of language in culture and society is to be assessed.* The boundaries of the

community within which communication is possible; the boundaries of the situations within which communication occurs; the means and purposes and patterns of selection, their structure and hierachy—all elements that constitute the communicative economy of a group, are conditioned, to be sure, by properties of the linguistic codes within the group, but are not controlled by them. The same linguistic means may be made to serve various ends; the same communicative ends may be served, linguistically, by various means. *Facets of the cultural values and beliefs, social institutions and forms, role and personalities, history and ecology of a community may have to be examined in their bearing on communicative events and patterns* (just as any aspect of a community's life may come to bear selectively on the study of kinship, sex, or role conflict). (*Foundations* 4; emphases mine)

Thus, in choosing the term "communication," Hymes married language to culture because he saw "the task of ethnography . . . as the discovery and explication of the rules for contextually appropriate behavior in a community or group; in other words, culture is what the individual needs to know to be a functional member of the community" (Saville-Troike 8). Thus the study of language becomes socially contextualized and communicative competence becomes imbedded in the larger notion of cultural competence (Saville-Troike 23). Again, according to Geertz, thinking becomes a series of metaphors used to impose meaning upon experience, and these metaphors are both language-specific and culture-specific.

These metaphors must be studied, according to Hymes's ethnography of communication, in three nested units: the communicative situation, the communicative event, and the communicative act. All these units point to the cultural imbeddedness of language in the sense that there needs to be a specific place, a specific ritual, and a specific behavior in order for communication to occur and meaning to be understood; in addition, the words lend themselves naturally to an extension of the Hymesean point of view as presented by Bauman and Sherzer. These researchers, in their exploration of various ways of speaking, stress the notion of performance. They call it a "nexus . . . between resources and individual competence, within the context of particular situations" (*Explorations* 7).

Sociologist Erving Goffman speaks of the power of performance as a function of the need people have for "impression management." Because his basic conception of social activity is in dramaturgical terms, Goffman defines performance as "all the activity of a given participant on a given occasion which serves to influence in any way any of the other participants" (*Presentation of Self* 15). This view leads him to speak of "the presentation of self" in terms of performances which can vary from complete veracity to complete duplicity. But, whether they are to be believed or not to be believed, Goffman stresses that all performances are roles— routines enacted by actors and engendered by specific fronts and settings to express and reaffirm the moral values of the community on whose "stage" they are played out. The question is not whether the performance is real or contrived because

> ordinary social intercourse is itself put together as a scene is put together, by the exchange of dramatically inflated actions, counteractions, and terminating replies. Scripts even in the hands of unpracticed players can come to life because life itself is a dramatically enacted thing. All the world is not, of course, a stage, but the crucial ways in which it isn't are not easy to specify. (*Presentation of Self* 72)

Goffman's theory makes plain that the way people present themselves is always a performance and that this performance is itself culturally learned. He implies, therefore, that actors and roles and settings are rituals which vary from community to community.

To the linguistic aspects of Goffman's "all the world's a [kind of] stage" view, Deborah Tannen adds prodigious insights. For her analysis she uses a framework called "discourse analysis"; in her definition discourse analysis is not a single theory or coherent set of theories. Moreover, the term does not describe a theoretical perspective or method-ological framework at all. It simply describes the object of study: language beyond the sentence. (*Talking Voices* 6)

Tannen builds upon Gumperz's insight that implicit understand-ings, or "conversational inferences," are based upon background assumptions which allow speakers to make sense of what is going on, thereby successfully creating conversational involvement. For example, she calls indirectness in discourse a possible ethnic marker of conversational style which is "more resistant to change than more apparent marks of ethnicity such as retention of the parents' or grandparents' language" (*Indirectness in Discourse* 236). Stubbs says that indirection is present in most uses of language, but that researchers can use estrangement devices (243) to understand how speakers achieve conversational coherence through inter-pretation (*Discourse Analysis* 228). Thus, discourse analysis can show how meaning is achieved. When cultural homogeneity is absent, Gumperz says, miscommunications can result. Tannen documents a whole world of such cross-cultural fiascos, including those which occur between men and women who, she maintains, are enculturated into distinct speech communities with different styles (*Gender and Conversational Interaction*, among others).

Tannen also explores those strategies which help to create successful involvement. Particularly important is her claim that "specific linguistic strategies have widely divergent potential meaning" (*Gender and Conversational Interaction* 165). For example, Tannen has described a speech style with overlapping turn-taking as "high-involvement." I see this style as typically Italian. Tan-nen's notion of "divergent potential meaning" allows us to re-think linguistic power and solidarity in such typically powerless strategies as indirectness and such typically powerful strategies as interruption. It also allows us to understand that language fre-quently has meanings beyond the linguistic level—and these meanings are culturally coded in performance.

But a performance is more than simply a link between the cultural group and the individual. To speak of performance at all is

to privilege the communicative act as separate from ordinary discourse, as having "an emergent quality" (Bauman 37) which dif-
ferentiates it from the language of everyday speech. This is not to
say that there cannot exist "spontaneous unscheduled optional
performance contexts of everyday life" (Bauman 28) but both performer and audience usually recognize them as such. In order to
single out the performer as a facile practitioner who knows how to
play to the audience, Bauman calls performance "verbal art as a
way of speaking" (5). Charles Briggs says that performers must be
"astute students of unique, ongoing social encounters" (20). Farr
discusses the verbal art of Mexican immigrant women in a performance called *echando relajo* ("joking or fooling around"). She
maintains that

> the self-expressions and self-assertion of these women
> during *relajo* plays an especially important part in the
> process of wider social change. First, it helps to relieve the
> tensions inherent in such social changes . . . It also . . .
> provid[es] a space in which changes in roles can be played
> with and explored together . . . validating them collec-
> tively, through humorous oral performances such as this
> one. (*Echando Relajo* 183)

So, while all of these theorists imply that performance is necessarily constituted by the mores of the social situation, it is also an individual feat which lends power to the person able to do it well.

The social context of communication in a bilingual speech
community complicates our notions of performance, for bilinguals
tend to have a greater awareness than do monolinguals of the arbi-
trary quality of language. Because their communicative competence extends to two separate codes, they also have a wider variety
of speech strategies at their disposal. Gumperz says:

> What distinguishes bilinguals from their monolingual
> neighbors is the juxtaposition of cultural forms: the
> awareness that their own mode of behavior is only one

of several possible modes, that style of communication affects the interpretation of what a speaker intends to communicate and that there are others with different communicative conventions and standards of evaluation that must not only be taken into account but that can also be imitated or mimicked for special communicative effect. (65)

This awareness means that bilinguals can build upon their alternative communicative conventions to lend variety and subtlety to what they say. One of the ways in which they do this is through code-switching, "the juxtaposition within the same speech exchange of passages of speech belonging to two different grammatical systems or subsystems" (Gumperz 59).

William Labov shows that particular choices in language use can be deliberate attempts to create and/or maintain identity. Sometimes code-switching can also be used in this way. That is, a bilingual can generate conversational inferences of solidarity by invoking notions of social identity implicit within the use of a particular in-group language. Especially in bilingual networks wherein this communicative option is understood, such rhetorical style can be very effective.

However, speakers can, for the most part, control the linguistic code of a language without having much notion of its cultural codes. Since cultural codes tend to be largely unconscious, even native speakers are probably unaware of them. Muriel Saville-Troike says, "Most individuals who can switch language codes with ease still use the gestures and proxemics of their native language, as well as its interactional strategies" (60). This would mean that native speakers of Italian with a built-in knowledge of the concept of *fare bella figura* could conceivably transfer that same concept when speaking in English.

In other words, while using fluent English as their language of communication, they could be performing *bella figura*. But if their audience is made up of native speakers of English who do not comprehend *bella figura*—even if they are fluent but not native speakers of Italian—this performance would be lost on them. The audience would understand the linguistic code of the message, but not the cultural one. In addition, as fluent speakers of English, they would probably not think they were missing anything. Therefore, the same potential for cross-cultural miscommunication can result even in the bilingual speech community if there exists real comprehension of the linguistic code but only ostensible comprehension of the cultural code. Such lack of comprehension is easily missed, however, because it operates at a less obvious level.

For example, I attended a committee meeting in which an Italian-born woman kept "interrupting" the American-born chairperson by talking to other Italian-born women while she was supposed to be paying attention to the official agenda. After the meeting, the American-born woman complained to me about the interrupter's "rudeness". The issue, of course, is that despite the fact that both were speaking English, only the American was attending to the cultural convention which demands attentive silence while the chairperson is speaking. The Italian was operating under another system in which either silence matters less[1] or—and this is more likely, in my opinion—determining where people were going to be seated was the more important cultural concern because it involves *bella figura*. In this case, attending to *bella figura*— albeit in English—separates the cultural insiders, the Italian-born women, from the outsider, the American-born person supposedly in charge.

Other factors enter into the relationship between language and culture. Class, for example (albeit an unwieldy concept for many Americans who like to view life as largely middle class), cannot be ignored, for it plays an important role in understanding the cultural semiotics of language. In my view, class is a construct which is country-specific; and, as such, it provides a way of looking at the world. In the United States class tends to be quite closely linked to economics, while in Italy a more important indicator seems to be how prestige (*rispetto*) operates in social stratification.

Anthropologist Sydel Silverman offers a useful description of

Central Italy which functions as a point of departure for under-standing its notions of class: Central Italy is essentially urban in its orientation. Despite previous anthropology which has considered all of Italy as a monolith, Silverman says that it is a mistake to speak of a Mediterranean homogeneity in which the social-class pattern depends upon being either a landowner or a peasant. Silverman finds an urban orientation and value system as well as stratification patterns that are quite different from those of Southern Italy. In particular she speaks of the contrast between towns-man and countryman as the basic status distinction, especially as expressed in relationship to living "within" (*dentro*) rather than "without" (*fuori*) the medieval walls of the town.

"The city is ultimately the source of all that is most highly prized by the society as a whole" ("Agricultural Organization" 16), Silverman says, and those whose participation in city life is re-stricted to special occasions—namely, the "cultivators"—are re-garded by all as outsiders. She creates a schema in which "the system of prestige stratification . . . can best be viewed in terms of three major categories, with six distinguishable groups in all . . . defined by certain contrasts between adjacent groups of the same dimension" ("An Ethnographic Approach" 907).

The schema works as follows:

A–1	—landowners
A–2	—professionals
	—white-collar workers and merchants
B	— village artisans, "civilized"
C–1	—village artisans, "noncivilized"
C–2	—unskilled nonagricultural workers, village
	—unskilled nonagricultural workers, country
C–3	—peasant proprietors and farm tenants
	—agricultural wage laborers
	—*mezzadria* peasants
	—drifters

In it the most important line of cleavage (symbolized by the bold-faced line), the gap between AB and C, is the contrast of village and countryside ("An Ethnographic Approach" 907–8, 916).

This notion is complicated by the fact that those who are considered "countrymen" do not always live in the country at this point; however, they still have a less "civilized" view of life than do the townspeople. So it is the "sphere of social interaction" (*Three Bells of Civilization* 68) which is crucial. In fact, Silverman lists the following as indicators for prestige stratification in the community of Colleverde.[2]

1. The level of *civiltá*. This concept, which can best be translated as "a civilized way of life," involves *edu-cazione* (not formal education, but genteel behavior), personal qualities such as courtesy and generosity, and above all conformity to a number of specifically urban patterns: fashionable clothing, nonrustic habitation, refined manners, nondialectal speech, participation in the cafe-and-piazza social life, and access (direct or indirect) to larger centers.

2. Occupation. Three dimensions are relevant: whether the occupation involves working the land, the amount of formal education or training it requires, and super-ordination or subordination to other persons and the position of the persons to whom one is superordinate or subordinate. (With reference to the third point, it is of interest that a crucial distinction given between government employees in A–2 and those in B is that the former originate orders at the local level, while those in B only execute the orders of others. At the very bottom of the system are the *garzoni*, who not only give orders to no one but take orders from the *mezzadri*, who in turn take orders from almost everyone else.)

3. *Istruzione*, the level of formal schooling attained.

4. Family name: the category with which the family has

historically been associated and the length of time the family has been in Colleverde.

5. Financial position. (The limited importance of this indicator is suggested by the fact that the wealthiest family in the community was assigned only to B. Their money, which was made in various commercial ventures during and after World War II, is being invested in part in *mezzadria* farms, and the wife uses some of the wealth in being a benevolent patroness to many individuals and to the community in general. However, even this translation of new wealth into traditional patterns is not sufficient to move the family into A–2. The families of A–2 who are the "*signori* of money," it should be noted, have all owned their land for at least one generation—but rarely more than two; longer ownership would tend to meet the A–1 criterion of "legitimacy by ancestry.")

6. Provenience from Colleverde. In the absence of any conclusive evidence of rank, coming from outside the community suggests a questionable background and tends to lower one's rank, at least temporarily. ("An Ethnographic Approach" 912–13)

This quality of *civiltá*—as gauged by how closely one is linked to the "city" and "city ways"—can be seen as at the very basis of all of these indicators. For example, if a person is not from Colleverde, then how can anyone judge his or her city orientation? Financial position is regarded as important primarily in relationship to length of association with the city; family name is the judge of this longevity in association. Even education and occupation are marked by the townsman/countryman distinction because what matters largely in these two categories is where one's sphere of influence lies. That is, education in general fits one for city ways and a job deemed *civile*. Thus, the *rispetto* accorded a Central Italian depends upon the level of prestige of his or her social interactions of *civiltá*.

Pierre Bourdieu tends to agree with this basic dichotomy described by Silverman. Bourdieu extends *civiltá* to encompass taste, the significance of which he sees as a sort of cultural capital functioning as a marker of class. In *A Social Critique of the Judgment of Taste* Bourdieu says, "Social class is not defined solely by a position in the relations of production, but by the class habitus which is 'normally' (i.e. with a high statistical probability) associated with that position" (372). In this way Bourdieu complicates class, for his use of the term *habitus* defies American conventional wisdom, which maintains that as people move up from the working class, they take on the characteristics of the middle-class "natives." Instead, Bourdieu maintains that even when people shift class because of economic gains, they carry with them habits of taste learned in their class of origin. In fact,

the specific effect of the taste for necessity, which never ceases to act, though unseen—because its action combines with that of necessity—is most clearly seen when it is, in a sense, operating out of phase, having survived the disappearance of the conditions which produced it. One sees examples in the behavior of some small craftsmen or businessmen who, as they themselves say, 'don't know how to spend the money they've earned', or of junior clerical workers, still attached to their peasant or working-class roots, who get as much satisfaction from calculating how much they have 'saved' by doing without a commodity or service (or 'doing it themselves') as they would have got from the thing itself, but who, equally, cannot ever purchase it without a painful sense of wasting money. (Bordieu 374)

In the case of the working class, "necessity imposes a taste for necessity which implies a form of adaptation to and consequently acceptance of the necessary, a resignation to the inevitable" (372). This means that because taste is circumscribed by what is realistically available in the real world, one learns to privilege the taste for the necessary by thinking of it as a potential choice rather than as a limitation. What is encouraged—often in the name of class solidarity as a rallying cry—is only what is economically and socially possible. In this way, group acceptance of necessity becomes played out as a virtue separate from any social and/or economic reality. Thus, what Bourdieu calls "the principle of conformity" becomes the language of those for whom "the universe of possibles is closed" (381) and their cultural codes are restricted to those of the countryman outside (*fuori*) the walls (380–81).

At this point in my argument, I repeat myself for emphasis: that language and culture are inextricably bound is the principal tenet of my conceptual framework, but culture remains primary. Hence, a summary follows of the various theoretical contexts—linguistic, sociolinguistic, sociological, ethnographic—which inform my conceptual framework:

1. The most important metaphor encoded in the social context of my language research is *fare bella figura*.
2. Both conversational inference and conversational involvement depend upon understanding the importance of and the performance of *bella figura*.
3. In a bilingual speech community where communicative competence includes a greater variety of strategies, *bella figura* can be performed in English, causing a potential for miscommunication with other English speakers who do not share an implicit understanding of *bella figura*.
4. Old understandings of class can restrict the ways in which *bella figura* can be performed but the importance of the metaphor remains constant.

Geertz says that ethnographic description is

interpretive of . . . the flow of social discourse; and the interpreting involved consists in trying to rescue the "said" of such discourse from its perishing occasions and fix it in perusable terms. . . . But there is, in addition, a fourth characteristic of such description, at least as I practice it: it is microscopic. (20–21)

This is how I practice it too, for with Geertz I believe that culture reveals itself in the particulars of time and place. Now, what remains to be explained of my conceptual framework is how these particulars are affected by a feminist frame of reference in language studies.

A History of Women's Language Studies

Sociolinguistic studies of women's language tend to center around social constructions of gender through language use: namely, how language is learned (Lakoff, Cameron, Goodwin, Maltz and Borker, McConnell-Ginet, Thorne and Henley); how power is related to gender (Eckert, Harding, Rosaldo, Fishman, all the pieces in *Locating Power*); and how linguistic miscommunication occurs, especially because of the andocentric bias of language studies (Bodine, Coates and Cameron, Graddol and Swann, Maltz and Borker). Even those studies which do not discuss gender as a specific cause for linguistic difference talk about an imbalance in social status linked, in my opinion, to gender. These studies explore how other factors—such as politeness, economic expediency, and custom—influence women's use of language (Brown, Keenan, Thorne, Henley and Kramarae, Nichols, Zimmerman and West) and how linguistic expression of identity causes language change (Nichols, Trudgill, Gal). Highlighted in the brief review of the literature which follows are various notions which speak of the relationship between gender and language, ideas of importance to an understanding of my Collandia Club ladies.

Many studies support the idea of lack of power as a basic issue in women's use of language, for everywhere male activities are regarded as predominantly important. Michelle Rosaldo traces this basic asymmetry to women's location in the private domain of home rather than the public workplace. This idea of the opposition between domestic and public does not determine cultural stereotypes, she says, but rather it underlies them. She also says it is significant that society views women as being effortlessly absorbed into womanhood—female adulthood is thus an ascribed status—whereas manhood has to be won or achieved. Something that has to be achieved is looked upon as a more arduous task and less natural. Harding's women in the Spanish village of Oreol, essentially powerless, develop a language of gossip that permits them a "place" in the town, even though this gossip also circumscribes their role by making them follow the same sort of rules they use to judge others. Having no real forum to determine their rights—the church and the state only litigate the disputes of men—women have just their tongues and the language of "finesse," which they develop out of a sort of desperate need to find authority for themselves. Women talk gossip, the "politics of the officially powerless" (Rosaldo 303), but men don't have to talk at all because they have the real power.

Penelope Eckert develops the interesting idea of "moral authority" as a way used by women to circumvent their social powerlessness. She says that boys who are part of a teen-aged group can engage in the activities that mark their membership, but girls have to rely upon their outward appearance of affiliation with "jocks" or "burn-outs." Therefore, girls assert their category identities through language more than boys because they are deprived of access to real power and have to settle for the best they can get.

It is useful to trace the notion of women's lack of power in psychological studies as well (Chodorow, Belenky et al). Carol Gilligan, for example, has created a workable set of metaphors—the female web versus the male ladder—for this purpose. A comparison of an eleven-year-old boy and an eleven-year-old girl, according to the Kohlberg scale of moral development, shows the girl to be less developed morally than the boy. Gilligan, however, traces this disparity to the fact that women's notions of morality depend upon an ethic of caring rather than upon the male notion of a hierarchy of rights. When the two children are given the same dilemma to consider—what should Heintz do about getting the medicine to his critically ill wife when he can't afford the price that the druggist wants him to pay—the girl answers in ways that seem simplistic. "Maybe they can talk," she says. "It wouldn't do the wife much good if the husband steals the medicine from the druggist only to end up in jail. Then how will she get to him if she needs him?" Gilligan concludes that, since women and their points of view were left out of the construction of the standards for moral development in the first place, their responses appear to be "deviant." When they are included at the outset, then their behavior can simply be viewed as another response to a thorny problem: they can be considered "different" rather than deficient.[3]

Gilligan's influence can be seen in Marjorie Goodwin, who shows the importance of gender to language development in same-sex groups of inner-city Philadelphia blacks. The boys accomplish their tasks in hierarchical ways in which the leader tells the others what to do. The girls, on the other hand, rarely use bald-faced commands, although if their rights are infringed upon, they can become fierce defenders of their territory. Generally, however, they issue suggestions in the form of "let's do this." These different linguistic approaches Goodwin regards as "systematic procedures through which a particular type of social organization can be created" (*He-Said-She-Said* 137). She does not view them as permanent gender differences.

Other interpretations agree with her. To look at sex differences as a binary opposition—that is, female use of language versus male use—is too simple a view of a problem that is more complicated. This research says that interpretations of language use depend upon an understanding of social context. Labov, for example, calls Martha's Vineyard an "island of r-pronouncers in a sea of r-lessness" precisely because he interprets the natives' language shift towards pronouncing "r" as a reaction against the Bostonian incursion to take over the island. (Bostonians delete many "r's" in speaking.) Peter Trudgill talks about the "covert" prestige implicit in working class speech norms as a leading indicator of change in Norwich. These studies indicate that identity forged within one's total social network is a (seemingly) more important determiner of language shift than gender.

Susan Gal and Patricia Nichols agree. While both their studies

show women making more linguistic changes towards the norm—
monolingual German in the one case, standard English in the
other—they explicate this change as motivated by reasons other
than gender. Gal shows that the bilingual women who live in
Oberwart choose not to use Hungarian even within the social
networks where it would be appropriate to do so, because they
have no desire to identify themselves with Hungarian men. These
men are peasants whom they do not wish to marry because of
their physically demanding lifestyle. German marks their affiliation
with the German-speaking monolinguals who work in town, who
are not peasants and who are the men they do wish to marry.
Therefore, because the Hungarian-speaking male peasants are
forced to go to neighboring German-speaking monolingual communities to find wives, the Hungarian language continues to be
increasingly lost as a linguistic choice in this town. According to
Gal, a desire to create a certain lifestyle or image of identity can be
seen as the reason why German is the language of ascendency.
Nichols shows how the black women on a South Carolina island
use less Creole in their speech because they have the most opportunity to leave the island for work. The men are able to stay home
and work with each other, so their Creole speech is perfectly appropriate for their communicative purposes. Nichols maintains
that social network is the factor which moves these women toward greater standardization in speech.

While I agree that to separate language use into categories of
female versus male is, in general, too simplistic, I also think that
greater weight needs to be attributed to the influence of gender.
That is, because they are women, Gal's bilinguals determine their
lifestyle through marriage and so their choice of language becomes
their class identity. Trudgill's working class men are the covert
leaders in speech style, not his working class women, whose
choice for prestige seems to lie in allying themselves with male
norms. Nichols, too, can be interpreted from the perspective of
gender in the sense that black women are viewed as less threatening than black men and so are able to get jobs which require them
to change to more standard speech.

If we attribute to language the power of the weaker version

of the Whorfian hypothesis—that is, that language can be at least reflective, if not constitutive of societal points of view—we continue to see female gender as inferior and sexism as institutionalized. According to Joan Swann, in the classroom boys are allowed dominance both because the teacher's "glance" goes towards them 60 percent of the time, thus encouraging them to speak, and because the girls in the class also expect them to be the first to talk. According to Don Zimmerman and Candace West, when men interrupt twice as often as women do, they replicate the power given to them by society. Women do the "shitwork" of interaction, says Fishman. Her studies show that in mixed company women do more asking of questions and more suggesting of topics, but also have less real control of topic choice and responses. So while they work harder at keeping the conversation going, their husbands are the real controllers of it. Elinor Keenan, too, shows that the "dirty work" of societal business is foisted on women. In Malagasy, in contrast to the United States, women are viewed as incapable of the indirect mode of speech, which is preferred and seen as the prerogative of men. So women use direct speech in performing the practical: they trade at the market, they ask Europeans for rides in cars, they yell at the boys who dirty the newly white-washed fences. Men, on the other hand, use indirect speech in performing the ritualistic: such as formal argumentation and wedding speeches. (Interestingly, the only time the men use the direct female form of speech is when they talk in French to their cows.)

Even more recent is the notion that to talk about women's language as some sort of monolithic entity is probably a misnomer. I agree, for the term denies the reality of more complicated concepts such as context. Regardless of recent research about women's gossip, which contends that "despite differences of age or class or ethnicity, women form a speech community" (Coates and Cameron 121), I don't think that women can simply be lumped together without any attention paid to their differences. Micaela DiLeonardo speaks of "the variety of ethnic experience" among Italian Americans in California because previous studies had focused on male, working class Italian Americans from the eastern

United States. Viv Edwards proves that female speakers of black patois are just as competent as male speakers, as long as they are equally well-integrated into the community. This research disputes Labov's notion of men as vernacular black speakers par excellence. Penelope Brown shows Mayan female "style" to be more than a conglomeration of surface features; rather, it is an attention to politeness and "face," which reflects social motivation.

Cameron and Coates say that women are always in a subordinate position, but I think that this subordinate position varies according to their race, class, and ethnicity. James C. Scott says, "Every subordinate group creates, out of its ordeal, a 'hidden transcript' that represents a critique of power spoken behind the back of the dominant" (xii). (Radner and Lanser refer to this hidden transcript as "strategies of coding.") Women have been, for years, a quintessential subordinate group, so it follows that their "hidden transcript" is to be investigated. I also think that there may be differences in their language when their audiences are all female. Therefore, the study of women's use of language in all-women groups—particularly when these groups reflect other races, classes, and ethnicity than Anglo-oriented mainstream white middle-class—is an area in which current research is necessary. It would seem especially important to investigate the intersections of gender and language within this specific social context.

Eckert and McConnell-Ginet agree. Complaining of "too much abstraction" in gender and language studies, they posit the construct of the "community of practice" adopted from Jean Lave and Etienne Wenger. This community is "an aggregate of people who come together around mutual engagement in some common endeavor" (95); it is not defined exclusively by population and/or location. Eckert and McConnell-Ginet's slogan, "Think practically and look locally," proposes abandonment of

> several assumptions common in gender and language studies: that gender works independently of other aspects of social identity and relations, that it "means" the same across communities, and that the linguistic manifestations of that meaning are also the same across communities. (91)

This rationale demands investigation of the specific social context of the Collandia Club. When it is viewed as a "community of practice," the important question becomes: How do language and gender come together here? The answer, I would claim, lies in the notion of performance. *Bella figura* is a performance of verbal art, a way of speaking; more than that, it is a way of being, of behaving, a legitimate way for Italian women to claim power in accordance with the norms of their culture.

Let us turn now to the Collandia Club itself for a description of that culture and its origins.

THREE

A History of the Collandia Club

Chicago's more than 500,000 Italians have been here since the 1850s. Most of them came from the "wave of unskilled Southern immigrants [who] came to the U.S. between 1880 and 1914" (Candeloro 229). These peasants "practiced *campanilismo*, living near others from the same village or region" (Candeloro 234). They worked as laborers, small peddlers, barbers, and shoemakers. They frequented settlement houses such as Hull House where they attended Americanization classes and learned to read and write English and vote. With World War II came possibilities for a college education and a house in the suburbs, especially as the old Little Italys faced the razing of urban renewal. By the 1970s and 1980s these Italian Americans showed both above average incomes and a symbolic identification with Italian ethnicity, especially as represented by *feste*, ethnic food, and many civic, religious and cultural institutions and organizations (Candeloro 242–46).

By then few spoke anything but English although they bought *Fra Noi* (Among Us), a monthly English language newspaper, which "in its 360 issues since 1960 . . . has reinforced a sense of Italianess and community among its 12,000 subscribers" (246). Some also read the now defunct *Il Progresso Italo-Americano*, whose demise several years ago signaled the end of a significant daily Italian-language national newspaper. Despite their concern with anti-Italian images in the Media—television shows such as *The Untouchables*, for example, and use of the word *Mafia* rather than "organized crime"[1]—they had arrived. They had achieved the Great American Dream.

Northern Italian immigrants, a much less numerous group, arrived both earlier and later. They were as clannish as the Southerners. (See figure 1, the map of Italy, for appropriate geographical nomenclature.) In 1871 some came to live on Chicago's North Side near the Northwest Terra Cotta Works where they worked as molders and, in 1910, in the foundries of National Malleable Grant Works in suburban Cicero. Rudolph Vecoli documents Lucchesi near "McComio's", their name for the McCormick Reaper Works in Chicago's Twelfth Ward in the late nineteenth century. "In time this colony . . . extended from Twenty-Second Street to Blue Island Avenue, and from Leavitt Street to Western Avenue with Oakley Avenue as its main thoroughfare" (*Chicago's Italians* 191). They continue to live there today. All these groups have produced a well-assimilated third and fourth generation.

After World War II, another wave of Lucchese immigration occurred, originally settling on the city's West Side, but dispersing in the late 1960s and early 1970s throughout the city and northwest suburbs. In general, the experiences of northern Italians were less difficult than the *miseria* felt by the southern masses who had arrived in the early 1900s. The post-World War II group was especially fortunate, arriving with literacy, job skills, and connections to Chicago.

It is important here to give a brief explanation of Italy's history and geography.[2] In 1948 the new constitution of Italy, now a parliamentary republic rather than a monarchy, divided the country into regions, provinces, and *comuni* ("municipalities"), each with an administrative role in the government. Italy's twenty regions[3] are much more distinct in identity than the fifty U.S. states. Before being assigned political status by the republic, they were historical and social entities for centuries; dialects as well as cuisine and custom vary from one to the other. In fact, Italians are likely to identify themselves by region as "*Siciliani*," for example, or "*Pugliesi*," especially if they come from small towns. Someone from Rome, on the other hand, would probably call himself, by his city name, a "*Romano*." Each region contains from two to eleven provinces; these take their names from the most important urban centers of the area. Within each province there are many

Legend:

    ●   = Lucca, the city

● ● ● ● ●   = Around Lucca – Province of Lucca

▬ ▬ ▬ ▬   = Around Toscana – Region of Toscana (Tuscany)

Figure 1.   Lucca, Toscana, and boundaries for Northern, Central, and Southern Italy

comuni. Comuni, in turn, are made up of *"frazioni"* ("fractions" of
the municipality) and *"paesi"* ("small towns").

Toscana ("Tuscany") is a north-central region which houses
the well-known cities of Pisa, Florence, and Siena. Also, within
Toscana is Lucca, a city of 87,000 which gives its name to the
province of thirty-five *comuni* for a total population of 377,101
(*Calendario Atlante De Agostini* 1994, 69–71). People from Lucca
call themselves either Toscani, the name of their region, or Lucchesi, the name of their province. Within the province itself Italians may refer to themselves by the exact name of their *paese*:
those from Barga would call themselves *Barghigiani*, for example.
Much local pride is associated with this naming process, which reflects centuries of heritage.

Many of these Toscani preserve their language, especially because the prestigious dialect they speak is very close to standard
Italian. The more educated think of Dante, Florence, and the Renaissance as theirs. However, regardless of education, almost all
Northern Italians tend to consider themselves different from Southern Italians, both in appearance—they are lighter, taller, more frequently blue-eyed—and in mindset—*Cosa Nostra* is not part of
their background; nor do they recognize an extended family of
commari or "godfathers" whose hands they must kiss. Their tendency is to identify with a Northern European point of view,
rather than with the so-called "primitive" South. Ironically, these
Toscani, geographically from North-Central Italy, are somewhat
looked down upon by the real Italian Northerners—that is, by
those from the extreme north of the country. Umberto Bossi, for
example, the leader of *La Lega*, the separatist party that wishes to
rid itself of all of Southern Italy, had to be convinced to include
Toscana within his costituency.[4]

This division between Northern and Southern Italy has historical, economic, political, and social roots, which are reflected
both here and abroad. In general, the division has been viewed as
a problem of Southerners. Since Italy's unification in 1861, the
South—known as the "mezzogiorno" or "noon" to indicate its
sunny quality and its geographical position—has always been
poorer and more cut off from sources of government help and

modern ideology than the richer North. (Even recent *Cassa per il Mezzogiorno* attempts to bolster industrial growth seemed only marginally successful.)[5] Historically, illiteracy rates have been higher, leading to exploitation of the many *contadini* by the few cynical upper-class landowners. This exploitation continued when Southern immigrants came to the United States—only now they were in the hands of the *padroni* who, "[a]ssuming the role of 'boss' and banker . . . imposed upon the ignorance and servility of the peasants of . . . [their] native province here as . . . [they] had in Italy" (Vecoli "Chicago's Italians" 248).

Redfield describes a fatalist attitude among these peasants, an unflattering "amoral familism," leading to "jealousies and feuds which frequently resulted in bloodshed" (Vecoli "Contadini in Chicago" 406). Historians cite a different moral code in the Mezzogiorno in general: family honor required that "dishonored" women marry their seducers; men were bound by the tradition of personal vengeance; and, in Sicily in particular, the code of *omertá*, or public silence before police authorities, thwarted government attempts to defeat the Mafia. Strangely enough despite this defiance, some say that there existed also a sort of mentality of subservience, a holdover from feudal society—perhaps the result of years of Spanish and Arab domination—which had largely disappeared in Northern Italy. Sometimes this subservience led to apathy.

Apart from the regionalism which already marked Italy and Italians—the country was, after all, a latecomer to unification—those Northern Italian immigrants who were already in the United States looked with disdain upon the Southern newcomers, who made up the largest incoming masses in the late 1800s and early 1900s. The Italian government contributed to an anti-Southern mentality by creating two sets of emigration statistics—one for the North and one for the South (Covello 29). The label of inferiority continues to this day. (See Cinel for an account of the differences in immigrants from Genoa, Lucca, Cosenza, and Palermo to San Francisco.)

Most of the United States probably has no comprehension of these elitist—if not racist—notions, continuing to think of anyone whose name ends in a vowel as the same kind of "Italian" or

"Italian American." In fact, public perception of Italian immigrants tends towards extremes of judgment. Either they are seen as *Mafiosi*, who ought to be feared—or as primitives, who should not be taken seriously. Even positive perceptions (ambitious people who have had the courage to leave their native land) frequently take on romantic overtones. Witness the following hyperbolic rhetoric in Lindberg's *Passport's Guide to Ethnic Chicago*:

> It has been said that in the heart of every man there is one small corner that is Italian. Some of the neighborhoods may be gone now, but the belief in spirituality, love of family, and the inner dignity Chicago's Italians hold will never be destroyed. (209)

In general, however, both immigration from Italy to Chicago and public concern with this phenomenon are now things of the past.[6] In fact, contemporary Italy now represents the "American Dream" for thousands of North Africans, Albanians, Filipinos/as, and Eastern Europeans who daily immigrate, frequently illegally, in search of a better life. Recent statistics (1997) show a million "official" immigrants, 83 percent concentrated in Northern and Central Italy, with perhaps just as many "*clandestini*" (Lonni 11–12).

Vestiges of Italian immigration to the United States remain in the abundance of voluntary associations that Dominic Candeloro says enriched the Italian communities of Chicago (239). In the highly selective process of immigration, according to John Mac-Donald, where whole towns were wiped out while whole others remained oddly untouched, these clubs remain as regional strongholds.

Such an ethnic group is the Collandia Club,[7] which was born in 1933, a comparatively late date for most immigrant clubs. (See figure 2 for the layout of the club.) Created by nine men who had left their province of Lucca, it allowed these homesick immigrants to "*[u]nirsi a loro agio, soddisfare così questi comuni sentimenti e rendere la loro esistenza meno monotona e penosa*"[8] ("get together at their leisure, to thus satisfy these common sentiments [the bond of growing up together] and render their lives less monotonous and

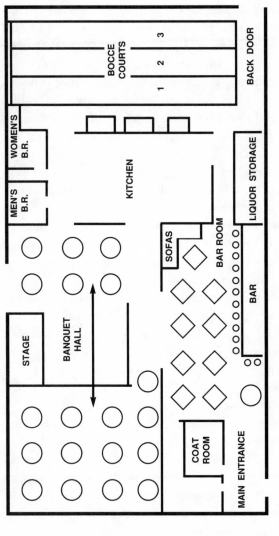

Figure 2. Layout of the Collandia Club

○ = Banquet tables
◇ = Card playing tables
□ = Booths

Ladies' Club meetings are held in the Banquet Hall.

difficult"). Throughout its history, the Collandia has faced the vagaries of many immigrant clubs: changes in location from small rented headquarters to larger rented headquarters to buildings that the club owns; long-awaited but problematic mergers with other, similar organizations; disputes about leadership; temporary member apathy. However, it has prevailed, establishing a series of rituals such as *"la festa campestre ed il banchetto e ballo annuale"*[9] ("the picnic and annual banquet and dance") which continue to be celebrated. Vecoli explains: "While the Italians had many contacts, especially in business with 'Americans,' their primary relationships of home, family, and friendship were largely confined within the bounds of *la colonia*" ("Chicago's Italians" 50). So it was for the Lucchesi at the Collandia.

Early on, the Lucchesi had begun to travel the world—it is often jokingly said that when Columbus discovered America, the first "native" he came upon was a Lucchese selling statues![10] Sensi-Isolani writes of the 300 year-old movement—both itinerant and immigrant—of the *figurinai* ("image-makers") which "scattered the inhabitants of a few villages to four continents, thus keeping alive entire mountain communities in the *Lucchesia*" (95). The "unique" aspect of this venture was its ability to change as the market changed, offering at first busts of Napoleon, then religious statuettes, depending upon varying decorative tastes. (Today they do a thriving business in plaster of paris nativity scenes, both in Italy and elsewhere.)

Italian publications herald the Lucchese business sense. Gugliemo Lera calls it *"per il commercio una spiccata attitudine"* ("a marked natural bent for commerce") (35). Marchetti cites *"l'arte sopraffina di 'tener bottega' "* ("the refined art of keeping shop") (19). Heilman mentions the tradition of an "economy based on small family-owned enterprises" in Tuscany, as well as in other regions of Central Italy (141). Part of what immigration provided for the mother Country was in the form of *"rimesse degli emigrati"* (stemming from the verb *rimettere*, the term *rimesse* means, literally, a "putting back", in this case, "remittances" of money to the homeland). So Lucchesi tended to thrive both in their adopted countries and in their homeland—where they have the well-earned reputation of being tight-fisted with their money.

Today, as a state-chartered, not-for-profit organization, the Collandia Club has grown, according to its bylaws, to almost three hundred "male persons aged 21 years and over . . . of good moral character." Every two years, these members elect a new administration of fifteen men; in addition, a nine-member board of directors, nine trustees, two legal advisors, and a club chaplain are appointed.

Financially, the Collandia Club is like a small "Big Business." Members pay a one-time initiation fee of $300—$1500 for a share in the club—and dues of $120 a year. In addition, banquets and parties for members and nonmembers bring in additional revenue. Real estate taxes for 1993 were over $10,000. In February of 1994 the treasury held a bank balance of $10,000, with total receipts for two months in excess of $59,000. While the president needs board-of-director approval if he spends more than $5,000, he usually gets it, because modifications and beautification projects are constant. No one seems to object to these reifications of *bella figura*. In the last three years, for example, the banquet and bar rooms have been refurbished complete with new furniture and pictures on the wall, the kitchen almost completely gutted and modernized, a new storage room added on, and a garden of evergreens and statues created.

The bylaws of the Collandia Club contain the following:

STATEMENT OF PURPOSES
The Collandia Club, Inc. is established as a social, charitable, educational and sporting club to provide for its members opportunity for friendly and social relationships and to afford to the members and their families facilities for their pleasure and enjoyment.

In order to preserve the American traditions to which this club is committed, the members pledge themselves to cooperate in worthy endeavors fostering a spirit of civic pride.[11]

While the club sponsors a Columbus Day Float, monthly birthday "*cenettas*" ("little dinners"), a Presidential Banquet, dinners for all the American holidays as well as other occasional festivities, the heart of the Collandia is quite simple. Lifetime friendships are formed and fostered here where, on a day-to-day basis, members come to play cards, to play bocce, and to speak Italian. Everyone knows about everyone else's troubles and pleasures. People get married, raise children and grandchildren, and grow old together. In some ways the Collandia represents the *caffe* and the *piazza* of the *paese* ("country town") that these men have left behind.

And what of their women? Historically, immigration studies have tended to discuss the "tensions between traditional values and New-World conditions" without much regard for female variation (Pozzetta 69).[12] Or—because family life is so central to Italian culture—they are viewed as the heart of the family, publicly silent while privately holding the purse strings and making important decisions (see Cornelisen, Yans-McLaughlin, Mancuso, Balancio, among others).[13] Only today are women immigration historians beginning to tell female tales.

These tales are complicated. According to Donna Gabaccia, "Migration to the United States was, as most historians now agree, an intricately organized social movement" (*From Sicily to Elizabeth Street* 57). She calls for common ground in immigration studies in order to encourage that interdisciplinary communication through which historians, sociologists, and anthropologists can discuss the study of immigrant women (*Seeking Common Ground* xi). In an essay in the same volume, Sydney Weinberg asks for research on "informal neighborhood and kin networks, created or maintained by women, and the effects they had upon the establishment of immigrant communities" (14). Carolyn Brettell and Patricia deBerjeois call immigrant women the "nodes" who are "frequently found at the center of these networks . . . [where] the significance of their actions is sometimes little recognized even by themselves" (47).

Such a network is the Collandia Club although an American feminist outsider would say that, for women, the Collandia "Ladies'" Club represents distinctly second-class citizenship. Membership is totally dependent upon marriage, "limited to the wives of the Collandia Club members" who pay $25 each year. (A widow can maintain her membership "providing she does not withdraw the initial $1,500 certificate" but she no longer receives some mailings because they go out in the men's names only.) According to the bylaws, the object of the Ladies' Club is

> to cooperate and help in the activities and financial programs of the Collandia Club, Inc. Our purpose is, like our Parent Division, CHARITABLE, SOCIAL, RECREATIONAL and utmost in our heart should be the fraternal love, respect and understanding for one another.

The women meet monthly from January to October, often on Wednesday evenings from 8:10 to about 9:45, during which time they have an official agenda and then have cake and coffee and play bingo. (Many women remain for several hours afterwards to chat and to play cards.) A typical meeting consists of the reading of the minutes, reports from the committees, old business, new business, and voting on issues of concern. The birthday women are always introduced and "Happy Birthday" sung, (a tribute to *bella figura*). Rarely is there a guest speaker. In the last two-and-one-half years, meetings have featured only three: a Mary Kay make-up consultant, a woman who spoke about self-defense, and a man who lectured on *Aida*. *Robert's Rules of Order* are followed under the supervision of the parliamentarian—an officer appointed for life who advises the president. All the officers sit at a round table near the microphone from which the president presides. The other women, usually about eighty, sit at eight large round tables, generally in the same places. There is always a hum of conversation while the meeting itself goes on, and sometimes the president raps her gavel for attention.

The Collandia Ladies' Club plans and manages three big "affairs" yearly from which they raise up to $5,000 each: the St. Joseph's Day Feast[14] in March, the fashion show in October, and the *Festa Fuori* ("outside party") in August. In addition, their Christmas Bazaar in November traditionally raises enough money for the Christmas party they put on for the members' children and grandchildren. They also have their own Christmas party. With the exception of the fashion show, these events, which usually host from 250 to 500, are held at the Collandia Clubhouse. Among the STANDING RULES, #8 says:

> At the end of the calendar year, December 31st, upon payment of the Annual Christmas Party expenses, a balance of $1,000 shall remain in the Collandia Club treasury. Any remaining sum of money beyond $1,000 shall be used for Collandia Club purposes.

It is important to understand that the term "Collandia Club" refers to the original men's group, so that this standing rule in effect tells the women that the money they have made must be turned over to the men. The language is gentle: "shall be used" does not say "will be appropriated by," but the intent is the same. This issue of who has control over the women's finances arises over and over.

It is also important to understand the actual make-up of the Collandia Ladies' Club. I shall refer sometimes to the general membership and sometimes to a core group which, as in all clubs, is the real heart of the organization. This core group is both official and unofficial. The president and her nine-member administration, the inner group with the official titles, changes every two years. The outer, unelected circle never changes: it consists of Toni and Sofia, two members who have been involved in all club activities for the last twenty years. Around them seven or eight other women, also members of long standing, flit in and out; sometimes these seven or eight favor the inner circle, sometimes the outer. In good times, both groups are in harmony. In bad times, much disagreement takes place on the phone and in individual gossip sessions. Rarely do confrontations occur publicly (*brutta figura!*) although the core group is always aware of what is going on. Generally, these conflicts have little to do with the men. Rather, they concern who has the power to make Ladies' Club decisions, especially to change the way things were done in the

past. Real or imagined entitlements (or the lack thereof) also cause
many conflicts.

Sometimes unhappy discussion results from the subordinate
role in which a few of the core group feel themselves. They must
get approval for their meeting dates; they must ask for the microphone which is locked in the front office. They must turn over
the substantial amounts of money they raise—as high as $15,000
in a year sometimes—to the men. They are also expected to perform the "wifely" functions of clean-up and decoration for the
men's affairs as well as for their own. While they, too, share the
camaraderie of life in the caffe and the piazza, they seem to be
conflicted sometimes about the emotional satisfaction that they
derive from it—not conflicted enough, however, to start their
own club.

However, there are many who do not grumble, who consider
that "to help the men" in unquestioning fashion is a worthy
proposition for Ladies' Club membership. These women tend to
be non-American born, non-officers, and over age sixty-five.
While they have some official status in the club—for example,
some serve on committees such as refreshments and raffle tickets
and some are peripheral members of the core group—they tend to
be more interested in seeing their friends (bella figura), eating
desserts, and playing bingo.

In his discussion of how ethnicity is symbolized in America,
Werner Sollors would say that these women side with "descent"
in the conflict between consent and descent, which he calls "the
central drama in American culture" (6). That is, these ladies see
the club as belonging by "relations of substance" to the men who,
as its heirs, are entitled to decide its rules. It is ironic that they do
not reject privilege based exclusively on descent, for Sollors claims
that this rejection of privilege is a hallmark of the American
national character to which immigrants lay claim. Despite the fact
that they are married to immigrants and are immigrants themselves, these women's Old-World views can be contrasted to the
American focus on "consent" as a determiner of individual fate.

There also exists a small but strong Italian-born nucleus in
their fifties and sixties who overtly accept the authority of the men

as "the way things are" but do much covert manipulating to accomplish whatever matters to them. Toni and Sofia, the leaders of the outer core group, are two of these women. Toni, the reservations person, is largely responsible for good attendance at the various functions; Sofia, the self-proclaimed arbitrer of how the club should be run, often becomes involved in conflicts by pointing out violations of tradition. They seem to be examples of Susan Carol Rogers' peasant women who actually wield considerable power while paying lip service to the "myth of male dominance" (752). Whenever they feel the need, they invoke the myth.[15]

The current Collandia Ladies' Club membership numbers 173. All these women live in middle or upper-middle class areas, about one-third in the city, one third in the northwest suburbs, one third in western or other suburbs. Almost all are homeowners with children, married to small businessmen, and most do not work outside the home. (There are exceptions: the widows and the childless tend to hold jobs; some women used to work but have retired due to age.) More than half of the members are over sixty; only one member is under thirty and she joined recently with a special dispensation from the Men's Club.[16] Perhaps three-fourths are Italian born, the great majority of these from Lucca, in particular from "*la Lucca f'ora*," the small towns which lie outside the city walls. Of the American-born women, almost all are of Italian (usually Lucchese) background with some significant exceptions: the president, for example, is an "honorary" Italian, for her background is Croatian and Scottish-English.[17] The first vice-president is of German extraction. Both are married to men with roots in Lucca.

The educational background of the members varies. Most of the Italian-born women over forty have five years of education because sixth, seventh, and eighth grade (known as *le medie*) only became the requirement in Italy in 1963. (Such an education renders them much more literate in Italian, a phonetic language, than would five years of American education.) The Italian-born women who came here in their childhood tend to have high school diplomas, as do their American-born counterparts; ten or so have some college training and/or degrees. Language ability varies as well; a few women are monolingual in English, a few monolingual in Italian, but the preponderance have mastery of both. Interestingly enough, meetings are always held in English even though the conversation at the tables may be in Italian. It is also quite usual to hear frequent code-switching and/or conversations where one person speaks Italian and the other responds in English.

Literacy is assumed. Signs of instruction, menus, results of bocce matches, and financial information are posted on the bulletin board in Italian, English, and a combination of the two. Minutes are kept and letters read out loud at meetings. Thank-you notes and birthday cards are regularly sent, bylaws published, special notices mailed out, written programs created. Extra copies of the Collandia newsletter and newspapers are out for people to peruse. A library of books donated by members is prominently kept under lock and key in the *bocciaio* (bocce court), although not many members seem to make use of it. Perhaps it serves a *bella figura* role.

These women tend to organize their social life around the Collandia. Many play bocce every Wednesday from October to April for $3 an evening; this sport, too, culminates in a banquet of 200 people or so. On the third Thursday of every month a *cenetta* ("little dinner") is held during which birthdays are officially celebrated (*bella figura*). Frequently women and their husbands drop in on Sunday evenings informally to play cards, bocce, and chat. Occasional outings on a rented bus go to the races, to the Botanical Gardens, and to plays. The Men's Club also has a banquet for every major holiday, including a picnic for the Fourth of July. It is possible to spend two or three evenings a week at the club.

There are some particularities many women share. A significant number, for example, do not drive so they depend upon their husbands or other members to get them to meetings. Many pay with cash rather than by check for dues, raffle tickets, and outside events. These are old-fashioned traits, left over from Italy when cars were few and where the use of checks for ordinary purchases is rare, even today. (Contemporary Italian women in their fifties and sixties do drive, however.)

But a concern for sophistication and *bella figura* exists as well. These ladies color their hair to camouflage the grey, paint their nails, and wear costly gold and diamond jewelry. Many travel yearly to Italy to see relatives and friends; along the way, they sometimes explore France or other neighboring European countries. A large group spends from late December to February in Florida; a smaller group visits Mexico; and another goes on a winter cruise. The food that much of the United States refers to as "gourmet"—namely Northern Italian cuisine—is cooked up daily for their families. They are, in fact, a notoriously difficult group to "feed": one of the routine concerns of the fashion show committee is finding a banquet hall where the food will not be complained about. One year's committee was particularly trepidatious about allowing the Greek-owned hall to serve *fettuccine all'alfredo*; fortunately, the dish went well and the women pronounced their approval.

About the Ladies' Club in general there exists a myth of gentility—perhaps another ramification of *bella figura*—to which both men and women publicly subscribe. When I was asked to write their history for the sixtieth anniversary banquet program booklet, this myth inhibited my writing. I appreciated the lively sincerity of my interviewees, but I knew instinctively that their tales could not be published even though my job was to produce a history from their information. I resolved the matter by "covering up the power politics" and, in so doing, "acting like a native."[18]

The phrases which I italicize in the following piece are those which seem at odds with the peaceful aura of "helpful Ladies' Auxiliary" which both the men and some of the women seem invested in maintaining. A deeper irony can be understood by hearing the tales that the founding members tell of a gradual progression from club independence to dependence.

The History of the Collandia Ladies' Club
by Gloria Nardini

The first Collandia Ladies' Club began with an organizational meeting at a restaurant in 1956. These founding women, *not all wives of Collandia members*, were either of Italian descent or *married to Italian men*. They called themselves the "Ladies' Auxiliary" and they were chartered by the state of Illinois as a not-for-profit organization. Their purpose, then as now, was *to assist the Men's Club*.

The first president was Elda N. whose basement accommodated the initial twenty or twenty-five members, including the current members Nora, Deloris, and Lorna. This original Auxiliary had annual dinner dances, card and bunco parties, and a children's Christmas party. During the Christmas season they collected edible gift packages and delivered them to nursing homes. Members recall with pleasure the "good times we used to have." Everyone lived on the west side, close to the club, and it was easy to get people together for weekly dances.

Meetings were held in English. "We had meetings, but if nobody ran, the original president took in again [sic] till she got tired," a former member said. Some of these C. Avenue presidents, besides Neddi, were Irma L., Ester P., Masie C., and Sara R. By all accounts, this original club was on a much smaller scale. However, despite their small budget, *the Auxiliary made gifts to the men*. In fact, there is mention in the February, 1963 *"Girovagando"* of *"la sezione femminile [la quale] ha regalato in occasione del santo natale 12 dozzine di bicchieri da Poncino, 6 dozzine di bicchieri da 'cocktails', una bellissima caffettiera di 75 tazze"* ("the female group which donated for Christmas twelve dozen *poncino* glasses, six dozen cocktail glasses, a beautiful 75-cup coffeemaker").

From 1956 to 1975 the clubhouse was on C. Avenue and 4th St. With the move to the suburbs, a two-week membership period was established; it allowed former members to re-join the club. After that, *membership was limited to wives of Collandia members*.

Sara R. was the last president from the original group. Upon her death Anne Marie A. took over, and she was responsible for initiating Italian Night as well as the Fashion Show and St. Joseph's Day. Many women of this era recall *meeting their husbands at the old club*. As teenagers they went to the Saturday night dances on C. Avenue.

With Anne Marie as president *the focus of the Ladies' Club changed*. Members started to raise greater sums of money, and they planned and programmed more complicated functions. For example, St. Joseph's Day had been a small celebration with the women bringing the food, but soon it developed into an event which netted $1,000. *This began the tradition that on St. Joseph's Day the women always give $1000 to the Men's Club.* Under Rina N.'s tenure the bazaar began with the purpose of funding the children's Christmas party. By-laws were also written at this time and official bookkeeping practices reinstituted.

The tradition continued. Liz R., beloved by all, fostered harmony. Ruth B. sewed as many Roman and Hawaiian night costumes as her decorative flair could create. She even improvised, she recalls, "at midnight a sheet for an emperor's toga." Pieranna C.'s fur coat raffles, *pentolaccia* and Halloween parties proved financially fruitful, and she continues to serve the club today with her St. Joseph's Day altar. Ollie R.'s ambition—to have an annual event for charity—gave us her dinner dance for Starlight Hospice, a successful first.

With Irene B., our "honorary" Italian, we end the list of presidents who bring the Collandia Ladies' Social Club to its 37th year.

My Deconstruction of the Myth

It is fascinating in deconstructing my rhetoric of *bella figura* to see how I, too, am complicit in the myth of female gentility. First of all, much of what my two seventy-year-old female informants said I left out. In the old club, they maintain, the women had control of the purse strings. This is no longer the case. Lorna said:

> The [original] Ladies' Club kept most of the money for itself. Our primary thing was to give the Christmas party for the kids. We never made much money. . . . Today it's a lot of money. The men didn't expect the money from us. If we bought something, that was okay. Oh, brother, is it different. Now they [the men] request the money. It makes me so mad.

Now, they say, the new women members have given over financial control. Lorna complained:

> Gloria, it seems as if they are so eager to give them [the men] the money that they pride themselves on it. What's wrong with these women? My husband tells us we're the biggest damn . . . I don't use language of any kind . . . but that's the word, the worst damn fools. He says that you have to hand all the money that you girls worked so hard to give to those men. . . . What do you have to give them the money for? Because they asked for it, because if you don't give anything, out. . . . I'm so mad I could spit sometimes. That's why I don't get up [to speak at meetings] because it gets my blood pressure up.

I gloss over this clearly stated (to me) conflict with the graceful, "Their purpose, then as now, was to assist the Men's Club" and "However, despite their small budget, the Auxiliary made gifts to the men."

The other issue which I left out has to do with entitlement. According to Deloris,

> They didn't want us in there. Maybe they didn't want us to know what was going on. Some of the wives called in the vice squad for the poker playing. Maybe they had that against us. With all the help we give them some of the men still don't want us in there.

Lorna said, "Men didn't encourage their wives to join, and a lot of women only spoke Italian so they didn't come in." Both admitted, "We could be shoved out of sight." I gloss over this sore spot about not being wanted in the old club by never mentioning it. Instead, I focus upon how the women created their own sense of entitlement: "These founding women, not all wives of Collandia members, were either of Italian descent or married to Italian men." This free access to membership changes dramatically in the new club, however, but I make no mention of any women losing

entitlement: "After that, membership was limited to wives of Collandia members." I also do not imply that any imposition by the
men caused this "limited membership," as is, in fact, the case told
to me by my informants.

In order to understand the accusation of second-class citizenship given by these two original members, it is important to realize that when the Ladies' Club began in the 1950s, most members
were Italian American women born in Chicago. To be the wife of
a Collandia Club member was not then a requisite for membership. In the 1970s younger Italian-born women joined in large
numbers. They were apparently more willing to allow the men's
club to dominate them. My rhetoric hides this new subservience:
"With Anne Marie as president the focus of the Ladies' Club
changed" and "Thus began the tradition that on St. Joseph's Day
the women always give $1,000 to the men's club."

But some of their casual remarks bespeak anger, too, even in
the "old" days. For example, many men resented women members, even in the "old" club, and some wives were angry at their
husbands' card playing, so they joined to spite the men. The most
telling comment, about being "shoved out of sight," may show
that things are not all that different from before. I write, "The tradition continued." Perhaps that "tradition" could be interpreted
to mean that in the Collandia Ladies' Club there has always been a
tension located in gender.

Ethnicity and The Function of Both Clubs

According to Joseph Venturelli, whose dissertation explores the
Toscani living near the McCormick Reaper plant, many members
of the third generation continue to live in this Northern Italian
oasis for sentimental reasons, such as parents and friends who live
close by. But, he says, "[I]f ethnicity includes the attachment to a
cultural group—its beliefs and practices, as well as the similarity of
conduct, such sentimental choices are laden with ethnic affinities"
(34). In other words, the geographical separateness of the area
functions as a "buffer zone" which "minimizes the impact of

American mass cultural values and allows the immigrant to assimi-late the surrounding culture slowly" (34).

But the Collandia Club is different from Venturelli's North-ern Italian oasis. It does not have a real community around it, an intact neighborhood where people live and shop as if they were in Italy. There is no travel bureau, no Italian American pharmacist, no local card and gift shop with Italian magazines and newspapers, no Toscano funeral director, no bakery to maintain the regional culinary diet, as in Venturelli's research area. In fact, the Collandia Club itself is an isolated building located on a busy street sur-rounded by light industry, commercial enterprises, the village hall, and its own parking lot. Other than the sign (which replicates the green, red, and white of the Italian flag) and the marble-like stat-ues outside, there is nothing here which says "Lucca."

I maintain, however, that its outside appearance belies the im-portance of what goes on inside where, certainly among the women, the "Lucca" of the 1950s continues to exist. It is a mis-take to call this group exclusively Italian American for, despite thirty and forty years spent living in Chicago, a familiarity with English, and an incorporation of American holidays, the underly-ing mores of Collandia are Italian. Conflicts tend to arise when this ethic is questioned by newer or more "American" members: women born in the States either accept the predominance of the Lucchese culture—in some ways frozen in time—or they drop out.[19] Some lip service is paid to finding ways to "continue" the Club through the participation of newer and younger members, but not many members really care.

Contrary to the common wisdom that ethnic "[c]lubs have changed their function through time, and the way people belong to them has also been transformed, following the vicissitudes of the 'colony' " (Schellenbaum 170), the Collandia remains largely unchanged. What is most important for these ladies is to continu-ally redefine and uphold their own realities. If we view memory as "very much a condensation in the present of past events" (Schel-lenbaum 159), then the Collandia has succeeded in an endeavor dear to many: keeping alive the "good old days." Living life here is a way to be Italian, including, of course, a way to *fare bella figura*.

FOUR

Bella Figura at the Collandia Club

If we view the Collandia Ladies' Club through Goffman's dramaturgical "frame," we can conclude that "what is going on here" is a series of culturally constructed plays: performances of *bella figura* where "actors" take on "roles" in which they make *bella figura* in specific "settings" of *bella figura*. While attention is also paid to avoiding *brutta figura*, this attention goes almost without saying. What matters at the Club—and it matters frequently above all else—is that any public appearance be one of artful grace and style. In fact, my "thick description" will show that the primacy of the Italian concept of *bella figura* within the Collandia Ladies' Club is expected, encouraged, and constituted.

Within the club, "routines" are established which create constant occasions for celebration and display. Birthdays are a case in point. At the monthly *"cenettas"* members get a free meal during their birthday month; their names are announced at the microphone, and the assembled throng sings "Happy Birthday" to a tape of the music. A photograph is taken of all of the women together and then of all the men. Frequently this picture appears in the Collandia Club newsletter where, in any case, mention is *always* made of monthly birthdays.

Full sheets of birthday cake are displayed on a banquet table set up in front of the podium and the microphone. This cake is specially ordered from an Italian bakery—unlike the meal, which is cooked at the Club—and contains an Italian-style custard mixture between layers of *pasta sfoglia*, a strudel-like dough, and myriad frosting decorations. It is interesting that the fact of bakery-provided cake replicates the custom in Italy where, despite

77

enormous feasts lovingly cooked by the women, the sweet will often be purchased. That is, if it is provided at all. Since the routine ending to an Italian meal is fruit, a sweet usually marks a celebration. It would seem to be the same at the Collandia Club.

The waitresses who serve the rest of the meal do not touch this cake; rather, Ladies' Club members appear in concert from all corners of the room to cut and serve it. Led by Toni who procures knife, paper plates, plastic forks, and trays from the kitchen, they pass the cake slices to the assembled well-wishers. All of this is done with little fanfare, almost in the form of a ritual. No one tells them when it's time. They just know. No one says, "Do you want to help?" They just do.

Birthdays are also celebrated during the weekly bocce tournament which meets from October through April on Wednesday evenings at 8:00 p.m. Women will take it upon themselves to bake something and bring it, saying after the game, "*Vieni, é il compleanno di* _____." ("Come, it's _____'s birthday.") At Christmastime little wrapped ornaments are presented to all the ladies, paid for with the $3 we contribute every week. There was one for the president as well, not a bocce player, as a public gesture of good will.

A collection was also taken up to buy both chairwomen a fruit bowl as a Christmas gift. Next week we found a basket of Hershey's kisses and a thank-you note expressing gratitude for "being appreciated." The chocolate thanked the women for the fruit bowl, which had thanked the original givers both for the ornament and for their organizational time. It seems that attention to *bella figura* requires that the circle of "strokes" never stop. The thank-you note is not sufficient because it does not display the reciprocation with appropriate flair. Individually wrapped kisses allow several treats for each bocce player, who then says, "thank you," again. In this way no one ever allows herself to be permanently beholden to or permanently bereft of appropriate display, for her gesture takes its place in an endless circle of other gestures devoted to sustaining *bella figura.*

Other gifts are also accorded scrupulous attention. Toni phoned to remind me that the club always gives its president a gift for her

birthday and for Christmas. The treasurer reported that $300—
surely more than a token amount—had been spent for last year's
president. Much ceremony was entailed in the presenting of
the birthday gift: a piece of expensive floral designer luggage was
hidden in the kitchen; it was pulled in on a serving cart to be presented at the end of the meeting as a surprise; within the suitcase
was a wrapped photograph of the president's first grandchild taken
immediately after birth. Everyone applauded when the president,
touched, shed a few tears. "My little boy! What a perfect gift!" she
said. This dazzling public scenario would seem to be in opposition
to the notion of "it's the thought that counts," a more commonly-
voiced sentiment in the United States.[1]

My field notes abound in attention paid to gifts. For example,
in preparation for a club shower for a member's future daughter-
in-law, one member had collected $40 from each guest. A smallish
sum, but the effect was going to be grand: a washer and dryer for
the lucky couple. Another example of appropriate recognition of
gifts hangs on an outdoor shed used to store tools, a fairly mun-
dane construction. Distinguishing it, however, is an engraved
brass plaque, which names the Ladies' Club president during
whose office it was erected. Last year the Ladies' Club bought
over two hundred new plush black and silver chairs for the dining
room; an earlier gift had been the three hundred settings of din-
nerware used for the banquets. Given the frequency of dinners
and meetings, such generosity is hard to miss.

At the 1992 Christmas party the Ladies' Club presented the
men with a check for $6,000, even though the ladies then had
trouble paying their own end-of-the year bills. Understanding
bella figura helps to explain why the ladies would readily accept this
otherwise untenuous fiscal position. Not only did the money have
a *bella figura* function: it was meant to help defray the costs of re-
modeling the banquet room. But the flourish with which they
were able to present the check—in a banquet room decorated for
Christmas, from the Ladies' Club president resplendent in a
beaded black dress and corsage to the Men's Club president in a
dark suit with boutonniere, after a meal of lobster and steak—
seemed to offset any concerns about being temporarily strapped

financially. The check was, after all, the largest amount ever presented by the women to the men in the history of the Ladies'
Club. Its presentation created a splendid spectacle.

It is also significant that much attention is paid to the wrapping of all gifts. For example, an important ritual involves getting
together to prepare, in assembly-line fashion, the children's
Christmas presents. These gifts are adorned with both paper and
carefully curled ribbon, which the children rip off with little ado.
(An annual event to which Ladies' Club members are entitled to
bring their children/grandchildren for a free gift, this festivity is
the subject of endless negotiating. Perhaps it is especially popular
just for this display of *bella figura* detail.)

The wrapping of items for the bazaar is also a matter of concern. At one meeting Nora gave specific instructions on the cakes
to be donated: "Wrap them attractively with plastic wrap . . . *Ora
questo qui ve lo ripeto in italiano . . . e quelle che portate il dolce, se
potete, incartatelo con questo plastic wrap con un bel nastrino che facci [sic]
figura . . .*" ("Now this I'm going to repeat in Italian. . . . and those
who are bringing a sweet, if you can, wrap it with this plastic wrap
and a pretty little bow so that it will *fare figura* . . ."). Nora's emphasis on how the cakes should be displayed assumes that they will
taste good. To make them saleable, she concentrates instead on
how they should look. A competent bilingual, her emphasis upon
bella figura depends upon her rhetorically self-conscious repeti-
tion/translation of her words into Italian. There is no comparable
term in English; code switching is essential to render the idea. So,
she renders in *bella figura* linguistic fashion a *bella figura* culinary
concern.

The meeting itself can be viewed as an especially public performance of *bella figura*. Toni phones me ahead of time to make
sure I know the names of the women who are bringing the cakes
so that they can be announced. Once when I was not home she
left a message on my answering machine in which she very slowly
and deliberately pronounced the Italian surnames for me: "*Ro-see-
march-ahn-tone-ee-oh, loo-ee-za–cah–pee-tah-nee-nee,*" etc. Further,
she said, "*se non li capisci, chiamami*" ("if you don't understand
them, call me"). The morning of the meeting she telephoned

again to make sure I had understood them. This despite the fact that she knows that I am literate in Italian, for I had helped her create a list of seating for *la festa fuori*. After watching carefully to see how I was writing the last names which were going to appear on a chart to be displayed for all the guests to see, she commented, "*L'italiano lo scrivi bene*" ("You write Italian well"). Apparently the announcing of the names is too important to ever be left to chance. When I said that I always announced the names one month late—that is, as the minutes of the previous month—she said, "That's ok as long as you announce."

Display upon display is publicly performed at every meeting. In fact, meetings are rarely over an hour in length because real business seems to be conducted informally on the phone so that at the meeting *bella figura* can be executed. Thank-you cards are read, both in English and in Italian; these acknowledge the plants and Mass cards which have been sent for illness or death. At the June meeting, in my role as secretary, I read the following thank-you note:

Carissime tutte
Ho ricevuto un bellissimo vaso, con belle piante e fiori, il mio grazie non sará mai abbastanza per tutto quanto, ma vi diró, e parte dal profondo del mio cuore, che voglio a tutte un mondo di bene e sono tanto felice quando sono assieme a voi. Un particolar grazie alla cara Deloris per il grosso disturbo, a tutte con affetto grazie,
Anna B.

[Dear everyone
I received a beautiful vase, with beautiful plants and flowers, my thanks will never be enough for all of this, but I will tell you and it comes from the deep regions of my heart, that I feel for all of you a world of affection and I am very happy when I am with you. A particular thank-you to dear Deloris for the big inconvenience, to everyone affectionately thank you,]
Anna B.

It is interesting to note that Anna B. was present during the reading of this thank-you, for she had sufficiently recuperated. But
she did not informally speak her thanks. Instead, at the end of
my reading there was a collective sigh of appreciation at the grace-
fulness and sincerity of her note. Several days later when I saw
Anna B., I told her (in Italian) what a lovely card it had been. "*Mi
piace come l'hai letto*," she said ("I liked how you read it"), acknowledging my part in the performance of the *bella figura*.

This reading of correspondence, which sometimes includes
other matters such as invitations or notifications, tends to occur
after the (brief) opening remarks of the president, which are
followed by the minutes and the treasurer's report. Both of these
reports often receive applause from the audience. Much of the old
and the new business is spent in public mention of the wonderful
jobs which committees have done or will do for the next social
event. After the 1992 fashion show, which earned a $5,000 profit,
the president said, "I think it made us *look very good*" (emphasis
mine). It is interesting that she did not say, "$5,000 is a handsome
profit!" or "The fashion show was a smashing success"; instead,
the rhetorical effect of "looking good" is almost an English translation of *fare bella figura*.

In addition, the names of the women whose birthdays occur
during the month of the meetings are announced and we all sing
happy birthday to them. This is separate from the fanfare accorded
them at the monthly *cenetta*; it happens at the end of the meeting,
after which they are allowed to go to the dessert and coffee table
ahead of everyone else. (Their names are, of course, recorded in
the minutes so that they are read back at the following month's
meeting.) Women who do not normally come to every meeting
sometimes appear, a little more dressed up than usual, when their
birthday is going to be announced.

Gaffes which arouse the indignation of the membership seem
to be centered around *brutta figura*. When I was co-chair of the
fashion show, called *serata dell'eleganza* ("Evening of Elegance"),
we forgot to buy flowers for the fashion show committee and the
president forgot to publicly introduce the past presidents of the
Ladies' Club. Both were traditions. Despite our handsome profit,

the lovely fashions, and the splendid meal, these *mancanze* ("lacks") did not go uncriticized. While any club officer might be criticized for forgetting to honor a tradition, these particular gaffes involve forgetting traditions which are pointedly display-oriented. Because the ritual was inappropriately observed, it was *brutta figura*.

In addition, one of the most important considerations for the fashion show had to do with seating. Toni, in charge of reservations for club functions since the 70s, insisted upon coming to see the banquet hall where the fashion show was going to be held. It was absolutely essential, she told me, that the tables be no more than two deep away from the runway or there would be "complaints." This positioning of the tables was so important that she asked me to leave the school where I taught—"*non c'e l'hai un'ora per lunch?*" ("don't you have an hour for lunch?")—so that I could meet her at the banquet hall where we would "supervise." Once there she amazed the manager by starting to physically move tables herself so that there would be a more equitable distribution of "good" tables. (Her action is especially remarkable because she has had spinal fusion surgery and continues to be plagued with arthritis all over her body. She is not supposed to pick up anything heavy.)

She also called "important" members ("important" means past presidents as well as very vocal complainers) to tell them that they needed to get their money in fast so she could assign them a good table. What is interesting here lies in Toni's interpretation of the word "good": it depends not just upon being able to see the fashion show well—that is, from up close—but also upon being able to be seen in a seat which others will also judge good. This means that the Collandia Club member's reputation, to a certain extent, hinges upon the position of her table, a visual display. Toni's actions and the ladies' implicit approval of them—the fact that no one else wanted anyone to complain about a bad table—are clearly dependent upon the concept of *bella figura*. In fact, despite a suggestion that tables be assigned "first come, first served," Toni continued to save some good tables for important club members.

Some years earlier a Ladies' Club president had invoked *bella figura* to outwit the Men's Club president, a well-known Italian

American who used the Collandia Club as his community power base. When he proposed that she and the previous president work together, Rina told him that he had to come to the club to announce himself that this co-presidency was what he wanted. Going to the Ladies' Club would have made him look bad—his outright verbal rejection of the president that the ladies had already voted on and approved would have created *brutta figura*—so he didn't appear. Rina knew that he would lose face by physically presenting himself, so she out-maneuvered him. Through her understanding of how important it was for him to avoid *brutta figura* at all costs, she won, so to speak, her right to the presidency. He "respected" her after that, she said, perhaps because they shared a common understanding of how to manipulate this potent cultural metaphor.

Another incident in which *brutta figura* figured prominently evidenced itself at a spring Ladies' Club meeting when the social secretary brought up for discussion an issue of entitlement. A former Ladies' Club member whose husband was still a member of the Men's Club had died. The Ladies' Club had not sent a floral piece, but there had been many unhappy comments made by the rank and file about this omission, which was widely regarded as an example of *brutta figura*. Deloris had thought she was following the rules as written in the bylaws. "If we're going to go by the bylaws, this is what it says," maintained Deloris, quoting verbatim the section which specified that flowers be sent only upon the death of a "member." Concerned for her part in having created the *brutta figura*, she wanted to hear everyone's opinion because "we cannot decide this [who is entitled to floral pieces] at the wake or the funeral—it makes for confusion."

At the meeting the president, who understood both how flowers represent a public display of club solidarity and how the bylaws allow decisions to be made in organized fashion, reiterated Deloris's request for consensus:

> We need to set some guidelines. I feel badly that Deloris was put in this position. I said, "Let us send a mass from the ladies.". . . her name wasn't in the directory . . . so it's

hard to decide. I know that families like to see that flowers have been sent by different organizations.

It was too late to change what had occurred, but many members were vocal in their protest. They would have been in favor of recognizing Nedda's death with a floral tribute. Her case evinced especial sympathy because she was only forty-nine. She had been sick for some years with cancer and had suffered heroically, they said. So the discussion centered around how they could have reified their sympathy with a *bella figura* gesture of flowers and followed the bylaws, too. There was a clear sense among the ladies that the two were in opposition to each other. There was also a clear sense that doing nothing for Nedda had been *brutta figura*.

One past president attempted a truce: "Even though she is not a member we have to bend the rules a little for moralistic [sic] reasons." Her solution would have been to send the flowers, using a case-by-case decision to justify them.

The current president felt guilty: "It's my fault. I don't mean to disregard members who have been around a long time, but I looked in the directory and she wasn't a member. Should we include past members who were in good standing?" She was trying hard to clarify the horns of the dilemma in a way that allowed both *figura* and bylaws to prevail.

Rina objected: "Do you know how many members we have that we never know the wives?" This was a clear vote in favor of the bylaws by another past president under whose administration they had been codified.

The current parliamentarian and writer of the bylaws cast her vote in favor of the floral piece: "Even though our bylaws don't stipulate . . . had her health been good I'm sure Nedda would have been here attending all the meetings and paying her dues. . . ." While it may initially seem surprising that the woman who wrote the bylaws is disregarding them, her decision can also be understood as wishing to avoid the *brutta figura* implicit in not acknowledging sympathy for misfortune.

Talk went on. When it became clear that the discussion was not solving the *figura* versus bylaws conundrum, the president made a bold gesture to resolve the question: she appealed to the strength of the past in order to forestall possible future gaffes. "I'm a new member and I really don't know—we need people who have been members for a while," she said about her brief affiliation with the Collandia Ladies' Club. She asked for three "old members" as volunteers to work with Delores, the Social Secretary. "It will be up to them to make a decision," she said. "I think we should have respect for *honorary* members."

Her creation and timely use of the new category "honorary member" was the brilliant stroke which resolved the issue of *bella figura* versus club bylaws/rules. For she neatly circumscribed the official entitlement inscribed in the bylaws by assigning a special kind of title—"honorary"—so that important gestures—"respect"—can still be attended to, in order to avoid making a *brutta figura*. This showed, I believe, her enculturation into the mores of the group, despite the fact that she is herself not Italian. She understands how *figura* has to do with "the proper order of rights and obligations in social relations" (*Three Bells* 40). It also shows how, on one of the few occasions in which a meeting departed from a vision of itself as a *bella figura* performance, it did not really depart all that far. The president was able to incorporate the bylaws into the cultural code of *bella figura* with artful grace, so that she herself (and the Ladies' Club, by extension) was rescued from a *brutta figura*.

Clearly, a dichotomy exists between how the bylaws encode *bella figura* and how it is constituted by the ladies themselves, especially at the meeting. Perhaps this is why what goes on at the Collandia Ladies' Club seems to have a life of its own. In fact, as my participant observation continued, it became increasingly apparent to me that an entire set of unwritten laws exists for what goes on at the Collandia Ladies' Club. I present them here.

The Real Rules of the Collandia Club

In the following analysis, I am focusing on the term of the president who served from January of 1992 to December of 1993, for it has provided me with most of my field notes. First, my purpose is to make explicit those tenets which govern what is going on at the Collandia Ladies' Club. Then, I will analyze the "real rules" from an emic point of view. This means that I will consider them in the cultural context of *bella figura*, specifically the gendered *bella figura* of women, most of whom were enculturated in the Lucca of the 1950s. My contention is that the more women understand and follow the "real rules" of the Collandia Club, the more they are able to create for themselves a sphere of influence which allows them to claim power. Their position confers power that is not necessarily formal as is the power contained in public authority structures such as the actual offices of the Club; rather, it is informal and covert power, apparent only through long-term participant observation. These powerful Collandia Ladies—who both make and heed the "real rules"—influence public opinion, control events, and in general decide that "what is going on here" is what should be going on.

There are two rules which have to do with the work ethic. The most important one seems to set the women into the framework of workers. It could be formulated:

Rule # 1—Be a Helper

Over and over I have heard the women say that everyone will come to help the evening of an event or at the last minute but few will take on the responsibility of being in charge or working on their own. One informant talked about how wonderfully well the women worked for the *festa fuori*, adding almost as an afterthought, "But you have to be there to direct them."

The ladies' preference seems to be for close supervision on a task-by-task basis. This holds true whenever there are craft projects to accomplish. For example, the person in charge will bring craft materials to be turned into Christmas ornaments and set up the task for the eight or nine committee women. Some will have done some work at home, and some will bring with them specific tools such as glue guns or staplers. Sometimes the few who drive will have picked up sundries from here and there, always carefully watching for bargains. In general, however, the committee contentedly takes orders and performs in piece-work fashion. An occasional woman might change the directions, but only after trying out the original method and finding it wanting—that is, still on a task-by-task basis rather than by viewing the job in more holistic fashion.

A few women engage in competition for the title of most creative. For example, some bring baby blankets they have knitted for others to admire, promising to show them how to do the same thing. At a bazaar meeting a past president said, "We want to do something different. *Ci vuole l'immaginazione*" ("Imagination is necessary"). Once one member of the bazaar committee made little reindeer earrings for everyone who had worked to create the items for sale; she carefully gave them out to each of us, doing so secretly so she wouldn't hurt the feelings of the women present who had not been part of the committee: "*Attenta, non ce le ho per tutte*," she said to justify the secrecy. ("Careful, I don't have enough for everybody.")

Toni is an exception to the above rule because she completely commands the job of table coordinator, even going so far as to phone people who have not responded to a particular event to ask them how many will be coming. She has a real system: lists of names, charts for seating, table numbers for the envelopes containing the tickets, and so forth. When she told me a story about how she thought (mistakenly) that she had misplaced tickets and money in the early years, I realized how carefully conceived her plan for seating is. "*Da quella volta non ho mai più portato una borsa al club per paura di confondere i soldi*," she said. ("From that time on I never brought a purse with me to the club because I was afraid I'd get the money mixed up with mine.") Perception of her eagerness and enterprise is encapsulated in the following comment, which most would agree to: "*Ci vuole una come lei in un club così.*" ("It's necessary to have someone like her in a club like this.") This speaks to her singularity in rising above worker status.

Even the physical configuration of the club contributes to this worker metaphor. The men play cards and/or sit and talk at the bar in the bar room while the women perform tasks in the banquet room. I have never seen men engaged in any of the same kinds of work and/or social amenities. Sometimes male members of the administration pay bills—in the office to which only they have keys—or meet in committee or tend bar, but they do not seem to "handle" artifacts. That is, they do not stuff mailings into envelopes or glue eyes on Christmas ornament dolls or take centerpieces out of storerooms to whisk away their dust before setting them on tables. Nor do they stand at the door collecting plates of cookies to redistribute on trays, one for each table. The men seem to be singularly free of things to do with their hands.

The correspondence for both clubs is handled virtually exclusively by the women. Not only do the women stuff envelopes, paste on labels, stamp and transport the mailings to the post office; they even write almost all letters, including those which report on Men's Club activities. One former president creates graphics on her computer to advertise upcoming events. On the Columbus Day printout, she put three ships with "Nina," "Pinta," and "Santa Maria" on them.

The second work-ethic-related rule, a corollary to the first, has to do with the quality of work the ladies produce. It could be stated:

Rule # 1a—When You Are a Helper, Work Hard

Jana said to me about an apron she had made for the bazaar, "Do you know how long it takes to sew this?" When I answered honestly, "No," she was taken aback since she had meant the question to be rhetorical. "Well, I really don't know," she answered. "I don't count up my time." But it was obvious from her demeanor that I had not responded properly; the appropriate response would have been, "Oh, yes, it must really be a time-consuming job." Because I am someone with little background in the crafts field, I took her literally, thus failing to give her the expected female solidarity response.

The notion of hard work extends into the bocce arena as well.

Sofia told me that I was *intenzionata* about playing bocce, which could be translated literally as "intentioned" meaning "serious." This is clearly a comment of approval. About my understanding of the bocce game, another player told me, also approvingly, "*Ci son tante che giuocano da anni e non l'hanno ancora capita*" ("There are many who have been playing for years who still don't get it").

Two rules pertain to money. The most important of them could be stated:

Rule # 2—Make as Much Money as You Can

For example, members are often encouraged to put together entire tables for banquets. Even though I was not part of the bocce group last year, I was asked to put together a table, and it is expected that I will do the same this year. When announcements are made about how much profit a function was able to make, cheers are loudest when the figure from the year before has been surpassed. This jubilation occurs despite the fact that the money is not earmarked for a specific use beforehand, and also despite the fact that the women frequently have little say in spending it. This year, for example, it went for the renovation of the clubhouse in amounts designated by the male president: the wallpaper, the new kitchen, the hood for over the stove. Sometimes the ladies have to be encouraged to spend it on things their group needs—for example, a microphone they can call their own. This mindset would seem to replicate the mentality in which the woman in the family puts her needs last and the "family" gets served first. Its corollary is:

Rule # 2a—Spend as Little Money as Possible

This rule gets put into effect when pricing objects for the bazaar, for example. There seems to be little value attributed to the amount of time it takes to make anything, for beautifully hand-crafted items are priced only according to what everyone thinks the ladies will spend for them. I have heard a woman who has expensive jewelry, clothing, and furs comment that she bought a decorative pillow for "only fifteen dollars" rather than the "twenty-five" asked for at the bazaar. She meant to encourage the committee to lower the price they intended to charge. Somehow this comment reveals a valuing of frugality that is separate from how much money members really have to spend.

Another way in which members "spend as little as possible" is by relying upon donations, even though the Collandia Club as a whole is relatively affluent. Many donations are sought for functions such as St. Joseph's Day, for example, where a local restaurant owner was asked to donate individual servings of butter, sugar, and cream; then he was praised for his generosity. Another member regularly supplies the club with cans of nuts from his business. Other regulars, particularly merchants who advertise in the newsletter, can be counted upon to provide raffle prizes; and no one is embarrassed to call upon them over and over again.

The ladies are also very hesitant to give any of their money to charity, even charities which benefit women and children. "Charity begins at home," Lana pointedly told me at one officers' meeting. "If we start giving to this one and that one, where will it end?" On another occasion, she had condemned the parsimoniousness of individual members of the group: "When are they going to learn? The kids are going to get it all—spend it!" These two points of view are not so irreconcilable if we consider that both imply that ownership of the finances goes to those who work for the money.

A rule which is a corollary both to the work ethic and to the mentality of frugality has to do with entitlement. It could be stated:

Rule # 3—Don't Freeload

This rule has to do with an equitable distribution of favors based upon the work put forth to deserve them. It is related to the women's attitude towards money that is implied in Rules #2 and #2A: when women "freeload," they claim dinners and/or gifts

for themselves and/or their grandchildren to which they are
not really entitled. For example, it seems that many years ago,
when everything was cheaper, a tradition began which established
both a Christmas party and a Christmas gift as gratis to each member. Since today the women's dues of $25 no longer cover these
costs, they are viewed as getting something for nothing (or
"freeloading").

But the heart of the interdiction has more to do with the
work ethic of the first two rules than it really has to do with
money. The women view the jobs they do as an entitlement to
privileges such as sitting at the best tables. Thus, it is in this way
that they are really "paid" for many tasks performed during the
year. Many comments center around members who are never
seen who appear to claim these rewards without having put forth
the necessary labor for them, thus "freeloading."

The issue of who is entitled is linked, it seems, to regular attendance as well. I was told, *"Da che ti sei fatta membra non sei mai
mancata"* ("Since you've become a member you have come to
everything"), indicating that my presence entitled me to consider-
ation. In any case, the members who matter are the ones who
come around. I have heard many times, *"E chi la vede mai?"*
("Whoever sees her?") as a sort of indication that she doesn't count.

Two other rules have to do with the importance of tradition.
The paramount issue here can be stated:

Rule # 4—Do Things the Established Way or,
Accept that "That's the Way Things Are"

For example, Toni said about the current president, *"É benvista. Se
ci hanno da ridire é sui cambiamenti"* ("She's well-liked. If they have
anything to say, it's about the changes she's made.") This is the
same Toni who makes it her business to telephone me to explain
(in Italian) both the history of the club and the way things have always been done. I used to flatter myself that she wanted to "en-
culturate" me because, as a recent member, I am eager to know
and my Italian is facile—and this is partially the case. However,

the president, too, is a recent member. Now I realize that, as the president's "best friend," I was also a mouthpiece for the conveying of unwritten traditions.

Sometimes this rule is more directly stated. Once when the president expressed ignorance of the way funeral flowers had been handled previously, she was told, "You ask. Why don't you ask when you don't know? You ask somebody who's been around a long time." Another past president, fluent in both languages, had started her term of office by conducting meetings in Italian. Then, "I asked them if they wanted English or Italian," she said, "but they told me meetings were *always* held in English." So she switched languages.

Tradition is also upheld in that everyone is expected to accept the conservative nature of the Ladies' Club membership. Attempts at change are averted by invoking a necessary fatalism. "They don't tell you to your face like I do," says one member referring to an objection she has raised overtly against a possible change in procedures. By means of such statements, she implies that not all the ladies have her verbal courage; they will criticize on the phone, not out loud at a meeting.

"These women don't go anywhere except to the club and home. They don't drive and those who do drive don't drive on expressways," says another woman. So she justifies her preference in restaurants which are nearby. This limits the possibilities to those restaurants which have always been patronized, of course, thus keeping things the same. "They won't like that," warns an officer, speaking against raising the price of the fashion show at the same time that she justifies her position as guardian of tradition.

This rule is, of course, linked to their relationship with the men. For the men do not accept change, either. The women's group has no real power or existence except as wives of the male members, but most of the women are fairly sanguine in their acceptance of this second-class citizenship. "We are here to help the men," I heard one Italian-born woman say at a fashion show meeting. Fairly typical of the feelings of many of the women present, her comment was not meant to be facetious. Ivana once told me that years ago the old men had objected to having women become part of the club, but *"senza le donne"* ("without the women") this club would be nowhere. Ivana's implication was that women held up the traditional social amenities, the cleaning, the correspondence, the general detail work important to any organization. She did not seem to be objecting to this role, but merely acknowledged its importance. Rina, easily one of the most outspoken of the members, defers to the men, too. "See," she said once when it became clear that as treasurer she would have to turn over all the money to the men without benefit of a reduction in the price for the women's party, "why do we want to get aggravated?"

Another idea which relates to how the women accept "the way things are" is even more primordial. It has to do with the fact that they must have husbands, for their only entry into membership is as wives. At one point it was suggested that "other" women be allowed membership—these others defined as young, unmarried women and widows. The conservative viewpoint of most was typified by one of the seventy-year-old members, who spoke on the telephone to me against *"queste povere vedove"* ("these poor widows") for whom she obviously had no sympathy. Her conservatism is particularly interesting because she has a sick husband and could be a *"vedova"* herself in the near future. Her sympathy, however, clearly went to those women who could claim entitlement through living husbands.

The issue of which language gets spoken is also linked to tradition. The unstated rule could be made explicit as:

Rule # 4a—Be Able to Understand Italian

Officers need to command fluent English—one member's explanation for choosing a possible candidate for the presidency is, "She's American and she can talk at the microphone." However, the heart of this club's business, the important conversations, go on in Italian. Many times during fluent conversations in English, women switch to Italian with deliberate self-consciousness. Once at an officers' meeting, for example, Ivana said, when explaining something she considered important, *"Ora questo te lo dico in italiano—cosí te lo dico meglio"* ("Now this I'm going to tell you in Italian because that way I'll tell you better"). Cora also code-switched because *"Questa storia é troppo importante per dirtelo in inglese"* ("This story is too important to tell you in English"). Offered by way of apology to the monolingual president, she blithely held forth with a complicated account of a marital relationship.

A final rule—and for me the most important because it took me a long time to learn—has to do with how things really get done. It could be stated:

Rule # 5—In Most Things, Be Indirect

"The real meeting goes on in the car going home," the president was told, explaining the hesitancy of many women to speak up at meetings but to comment afterwards in private. Frequently Toni and Rina have said, "I got so many phone calls about that!" referring to an unpopular decision that was not protested against officially at the meeting. (I have often regarded the ladies' use of the telephone as a private act, almost in opposition to what they regard as the public use of the microphone. The latter is seen as threatening and demanding the English language, the former as warmly intimate and conducive to the speaking of Italian.) At one meeting the past president stated overtly, "Sometimes we have to bend the rules" in referring to who should be the recipient of funeral flowers. This is the same woman about whom Jeanne said, "She believes you catch more flies with honey . . . me—I just say what I mean." Cora once told me when I was unhappy about the disagreement between two members, "Smile *e di' di si e poi fai come credi*" ("Smile and say 'yes' and then do what you think best").

About their habit of indirection, a member of the nominating committee remarked ruefully, "How could I forget—when Italians say 'no' they mean 'yes!' " when she told me about a member's hurt feelings at being "passed over" for an office. The nominating committee chairperson, born and raised in the U.S., had not insisted that the Italian-born member accept a particular office, taking her initial "no" as her real answer. Later, of course, when she found out that the member was upset, she remembered the cultural difference.[2]

My Blunders before I Knew the "Real" Rules

In fact, when I remember how I approached the first task I took on—being co-chair of the fashion show—I realize I broke just about every unspoken rule the Collandia Club has. Disregarding "Do Things the Established Way," the co-chair and I decided to change the organization of the fashion show: Toni would not be in charge of seating people; seating would be "first come, first served." Disregarding "Make as Much Money as You Can," we suggested that some of the money we made go to a charity for women. Disregarding "Spend as Little as Possible," we vowed to make the evening elegant even if that cost more money than usual—for example, having a harpist during the cocktail hour.

After our first committee meeting there followed days of upset in which members reported to other members unconventionalities that the fashion show committee was considering. The president was told that someone who was a member of the committee was going to drop out because we had ignored Toni's "*lavoro*" ("work"). This would have been an effective protest against our failure to recognize that Toni obeyed "When You Are a Helper, Work Hard." We were criticized for wanting to donate money to a charity, disregarding "Be a Helper," when the reason that the Ladies' Club existed was to help the men, who had plenty of expenses coming up in refurbishing the clubhouse. The implication was: Who did we think we were, upstart members with no respect for how everything had been handled in the past? We apparently did not know how to respect "That's Just the Way Things Are."

Not all of these unhappy decisions were consciously anti-tradition. For example, in not understanding the importance of ritual, the president and I did not ask how the program had been set up before—thereby forgetting to announce the presence of former presidents at the show itself. Unmindful of the importance of everyone's sense of display, when a committee member said that she didn't want to model a fur coat, we did not insist that she meet us at the furrier's. On the morning after the show, however, we received a telephone call from her in which she criticized decisions we had made. In particular, she objected to how "silly" some of the women looked modeling such "funny" furs. Initially, I felt disheartened for I had worked so hard and thought that the evening was a success. It only dawned on me much later that she felt hurt. She was giving vent to feelings of having been overlooked in the public *bella figura* of the other women who paraded down the runway. Throughout the year she had obeyed the dictate "Don't Freeload," but we had failed to reward her by insisting that she take what she was entitled to, namely, a part in the performance.

Enculturation At Last

Months later the President and I negotiated a coup by means of indirection; its success can be attributed to our understanding of its subtle processes at the Collandia.[3] A friend of ours, a woman who was dealing with delicate family problems, wanted to begin attending club meetings. Despite the fact that her husband had been a member for years, she had heretofore ignored Ladies' Club membership. The deadline for membership had passed, however, and we were not sure how to handle what we saw as our friend's pressing need as opposed to the Collandia Club bylaws (and public feeling that, in this case, the bylaws were right.)

Then we conceived of a plan—on the telephone, of course. Together, the president and I called Toni, who had an inkling of our friend's problems, to tell her that Bettina wanted to join. We weren't sure how to get her past the bylaws, we said, knowing Toni's antipathy for what she saw as the formal trouble caused by the bylaws. But we wanted her to be able to be a member right away, rather than having to wait until till January of the next year.

She *needed* some time away from the house *now*, we entreated. Perhaps we should call the treasurer and explain the situation.

Toni agreed, whereupon we made a phone call to the treasurer, explaining Bettina's plight as "needing to get out of the house." "Just have her date the check March 30th," the treasurer decided, "and I'll say I didn't get it till later." Elated, the president and I phoned our friend to tell her how to date her check "for bookkeeping purposes," and Bettina was announced as a new member in April.

What a striking difference between this self-conscious and much more easily negotiated performance and our awkward misunderstandings described earlier! Two women, friends of long standing, both enculturated in DIRECTION, had learned to be indirect when the situation called for it. To this day we reminisce about how we learned.

The "Real" Rules as a Whole

To summarize how the Collandia Club Ladies really behave within the confines of their Club, I repeat my understanding of their cultural code:

> RULE #1 — Be a Helper
> RULE #1a—When You are a Helper, Work Hard
> RULE #2 — Make as Much Money as You Can
> RULE #2a—Spend as Little Money as Possible
> RULE #3 — Don't Freeload
> RULE #4 — Do Things the Established Way or Accept That
>   "That's the Way Things Are"
> RULE #4a—Be Able to Understand Italian
> RULE #5 — In Most Things, Be Indirect

What is the relationship of these rules to each other?

Issues of culture, gender, class and power are intertwined among them all. Because these rules can be applied to the making and furthering of a good impression, all may be viewed as ways of publicly creating *bella figura* and publicly avoiding *brutta figura*. For example, women pay attention to decoration; they also look good by working hard. The work itself shows appropriate devotion to home and family. People are hierarchically positioned and attendance is important, thus furthering attention to visibility. In this the rules are distinctly Italian in origin, even to the use of Italian as a primary (albeit unofficial) language. Since I perceive these rules to be the "real" way the Collandia Club operates, we can say that at the Collandia Club ramifications of entitlement depend upon a clear understanding of *bella figura*. While the ladies do not necessarily need to be born in Italy, they need to understand that those who do *bella figura* well and summarily avoid *brutta figura* are the ones who hold the power. In this enterprise they are buffeted by the years of tradition which undergird the Italian cultural construction as a public manifestation. Thus, the link between culture and power which obtains in this society lies in the overarching and public concept of *fare bella figura*.[4]

Among the women, however, this notion of public *figura* seems to depend upon a private understanding that is seldom voiced. That is, while the Collandia Club "real rules" seem to depend upon a public view of power as traditionally in the hands of men, in reality the ladies have their own private world with its own private rules for power. That is, the performance of *bella figura* is public; while underneath, their own wielding of power is private. That this power is also substantial probably explains why indirection is an important strategy for its maintenance: indirection mitigates possible confrontations that might create *brutta figura*. White middle-class Americans, especially those who are Anglo and male or enculturated in ways similar to Anglo males, may see this indirection as "manipulative," but it is not necessarily so intended by the Collandia ladies.[5] Indirection is also frequently viewed as a characteristic of submissive people; but, according to Tannen, it is "not in itself a strategy of subordination. Rather, it can be used by either the powerful or the powerless" ("The Relativity of Linguistic Strategies" 175).

In fact, as explained by Susan Carol Rogers, the model for this society is quintessentially peasant-like, especially in its use of indirection. Rogers, who did ethnographic research in the Lorraine valley of France in a peasant town she calls "G.F.," describes power relationships there as "nonhierarchical." This implies that power can be held by both men and women provided that certain criteria are met to satisfy both: that is, according to Rogers, the "myth" of male dominance must be adhered to by both sexes, at least in public. The men can hold the appearance of power—both in the French village or here in the Collandia Club—as long as the women pay lip service to the fact that the men make all the decisions. At the same time, the women can hold the actual power as long as they engage in upholding ostensible subservience to their husbands. This myth is expressed in patterns of public deference towards men as well as in the men's monopolization of positions of authority and prestige. Each group really wins, in the long run: both pretend that the myth of male dominance is the reality—because it is in their best interests to maintain the myth—while their actual behavior frequently shows otherwise.

I do not think that conditions here are the same as in "G.F."—for one, the Collandia Club is really primarily a Men's Club, begun by men and run by male members who pay larger fees to join and to maintain their membership than do the women. Therefore, it makes sense that they dispose of these funds as they see fit. But I do think that women hold much more power in the club than is apparent at first. This is because the Collandia Club has a mindset which is like Rogers' peasant village behaviorally and ideologically in many ways.

First of all, both groups of women make money. The Collandia ladies, while not in charge of a primary economic unit such as the produce of the farm, make impressive sums yearly in fundraising events for the men. The figure might be as high as $20,000, even though this amount is not written down anywhere, because the women help financially in ways which are less overt than gifts of $6,000 at Christmastime and $1000 for St. Joseph's Day. Besides the fashion show, which is held elsewhere and brings in about $5,000 in clear profit, their other functions are held at the club itself. This means that profit is not just what they hand the men in the form of a big check, but also the percentage which the men make from every dinner eaten at the club.

The Ladies' Club contributes untold amounts of free labor, which also has a direct financial return. Women send out information about monthly *cenettas*, thereby increasing attendance at them. They provide the husbands of the women's members with a free Christmas dinner, their children and grandchildren with a free Christmas party; these parties are paid for with profits from the women's Christmas bazaar. They also render other banquets more pleasant by decorating the tables and the room, baking homemade desserts, donating baskets to be raffled off, and so forth. They procure ads for ad books and donations of food and services, provide free cleaning services, replenish dishes and glasses when necessary, etc. It is impossible to really measure accurately the amount of money they bring in, for some of it depends upon their acting as a sort of moral force. For example, would the men even attend the club's events as regularly if they didn't have the approval and/or encouragement of their wives?

Both male and female members talk about the women's role as "helping the men." In many ways, this phrase is a euphemism for "making money." Despite the indirection evident in their bylaws, which allow them to "keep" $1000 from year to year, the very fact that this rule is listed is a tacit acknowledgment of the importance of the women's ability to make money. This is really how they help the men. In fact, on one male president's Collandia Club statement of cash receipts and disbursements, there is a section marked "Contributions; Ladies Auxil." under "Receipts." That this is a printed line, along with "Bar & Banquets," Membership, Dues, Advertisers, Bulletin and other listings of possible revenues, indicates that what the Ladies' Club produces is an expected and regular source of revenue.

Many of the Collandia Club women have maintained earlier notions of frugality and cleverness in the handling of money despite the increased affluence afforded them by immigration to the United States. The Bourdieuian notion of *habitus* is important here, for these are women used to physical work; their ideology about what they can have limits them to the possible, to spending only what is necessary. They have also learned a sort of female indirection, similar to what Rogers describes, in which they tend to manipulate the apparently male-oriented formal system to suit their own ends. That is, while they pay appropriate deference to the fact that this is a Men's Club, they also tend to say and do more or less what they want when they are on their own. They also have very definite rules governing what counts for appropriate behavior (i.e., a *bella figura* performance) among the women. Therefore, we cannot assume that because they seem powerless, they really have no power. Once again, the link between gender and power lies in the overarching and public concept of *fare bella figura* as manipulated by women enculturated by ethnicity and by class to indirection.

DiLeonardo maintains that women's work operates in three spheres: the home, which involves housework and child care; paid labor in the outside marketplace; and, a new concept introduced by her, "the work of kinship" which she defines as:

> the conception, maintenance, and ritual celebration of cross-household kin ties, including visits, letters, telephone calls, presents, and cards to kin; the organization of holiday gatherings; the creation and maintenance of quasi-kin relations; decisions to neglect or to intensify particular ties; the mental work of reflection about all these activities; and the creation and communication of altering images of family and kin vis-à-vis the images of others, both folk and mass media. ("The Female World" 442-43)

Notice how DiLeonardo's words can be linked to *bella figura*. When she speaks of "the creation and communication of *altering images* of family and kin vis-a-vis the images of others, both *folk and mass media*," she is referring to appearances and the part that women play in managing them. Notice also that these are duties difficult to define, rarely done by men, and dependent upon negotiation, the same sort of activities in which we see the Collandia

Ladies' Club engaged. It is certainly possible then to think of the Collandia Club as a quasi-kin network in which women "undertake labor in order to create obligations in men and children and to gain power over one another" ("The Female World" 451). In fact, this would seem to give club membership an important reason for existence, for through it these women define and re-define their own realities.

Because *fare bella figura* is a public concept, it depends for its enactment upon display and performance. The paradox, however, is that for male dominance to work as a myth, women must perform indirectly. Thus, much lip service is paid to "helping the men," while private constructions of power remain underground and largely unremarked. Therefore, while it may seem that the women have little power of their own, such an explanation works only upon the surface, for it ignores the fact that the workings of the Collandia Club depend upon a fine-tuned balance between public and private, male and female, myth and reality. In short, a performance of *bella figura*.

FIVE

The Transcript: A Linguistic Event
Transformed by *Bella Figura*

In this chapter I will present an example of the performance of *bella figura*; I have analyzed a partial transcript of a Collandia Ladies' Club Officers' meeting using methodology formulated by Hymes, Saville-Troike, Tannen, and Stubbs. The following questions will be answered:

—What is the social context of this interaction? That is: How do these women present themselves? How are they members of the same speech community?

—What are the communicative strategies at work here? How do they create conversational involvement?

—Where does performance occur? How is this an example of a performance which is communally constituted?

—What role does indirection and the view of women as powerless users of language play in this discourse?

Geertz says that culture reveals itself in particulars of time and place, so the overarching question—again—of this analysis remains: How are language and culture inextricably bound? I maintain that in this transcript the Collandia Ladies claim social power for themselves through their linguistic use of *bella figura*. Thus, our interpretation of their ways of speaking, both gendered and culture-rich, is dependent upon the social context of the Collandia Club for its full meaning.

(Please refer to Appendix A for the transcript which I describe below. You may wish to read through all of it now. As I go along, I will also incorporate portions of this transcript into my explanatory text.)

To use Hymesean terms, in this communicative situation,

otherwise known as the end-of-the-year Collandia Ladies' Club officers' financial meeting, a communicative event takes place: the women ask the Men's Club president for a reduction in Ladies' Club debt as they attend to the task of finalizing their 1992 books. Within this event occur discrete communicative acts; specifically, a series of perfomances, one of which I define as a starring moment. This dazzling act is a performance of *bella figura* by the Ladies' Club treasurer.

To analyze the communicative event requires that attention be paid to its salient components, says Saville-Troike, who also maintains that:

> The criterion for descriptive adequacy . . . is that enough information should be provided to enable someone from outside the speech community under investigation to fully understand the event, and to participate appropriately in it. (119)

In the following description, I shall italicize Saville-Troike's terminology as I explicate its particulars vis-à-vis my transcript. She speaks of *scene* as being composed of *genre, topic, purpose/function*, and *setting*. In this case, the *genre* is persuasive discourse. Rina, the treasurer, wants the ladies to help her convince Ciro, the Men's Club president, that the women owe less money than is actually shown in their books. There are two reasons for this, Rina maintains: first, the Ladies' Club paid for expenses which, by rights, do not belong to them and for which the Men's Club should reimburse them; second, they were not reimbursed even for bills, such as the stamps used on New Year's Eve mailings, for which the Men's Club does accept responsibility. Therefore, instead of paying the total which they owe to the Collandia for the Ladies' Christmas Party, Rina wants Ciro to acknowledge those expenses which belong to the Men's Club so she can deduct them from what the ladies owe. Thus, her *topic, purpose*, and *function* are to straighten out who is responsible for what expenses so that efficient payment can be made.

The setting for this meeting, always held in late December or early January, is the banquet room of the clubhouse with the ladies seated at a round table; copies of the treasurer's report are spread out in front of them. At this point in the conversation, having clarified their finances for themselves, the women are clearly waiting for the Men's Club president to meet with them. When Ciro enters, he participates from a standing position next to the seated ladies.

Next, the participants. (Please refer to figure 3 for an explanation of their characteristics, including their attitudes towards resolving the gender conflicts implicit within the Collandia Club.) Nine women are present, although in this particular segment of the transcript only eight of them speak. Five of them are American-born, three of these of parents born in Lucca. All three of these women understand Italian and two speak it with near-native fluency, one of these two having used Italian as a primary language before she went to school. The other two American-born women are of non-Italian background; one comes from German parents and was raised on a Wisconsin farm, the other from American-born parents of Croatian, English, and Scottish heritage who raised her in Chicago. Both are married to bilingual Lucchese men but neither one understands much Italian other than simple phrases, food words, greetings, etc. They both, however, have identified themselves strongly with the Collandia Club and with the Italian community in general. They have traveled to Italy and keep up with their husband's relatives there. They have many Italian-speaking friends. One is the current president and the other the first vice-president of the Ladies' Club.

Of the four Italian-born women, three are Lucchesi. Two of these women came here as children: one was nine and the other twelve. Their English, while slightly accented, is near-native in proficiency. The other two, who emigrated in their twenties, have no difficulty understanding English although one is more proficient in spoken English than the other. These women know each other well.

All of the American-born women have at least a high school diploma as do two of the Italian-born women. There is not anyone here who has not held a job, although only three are currently

Table 1. The Participants in the Transcript

Name	Office	Philosophy of Gender Equity[1]	Age/ Birthplace	Languages	Job
Rina	treasurer	F-SCR-why?	50s, Lucca	f/b, 12	doctor's office
Frida	trustee	do it right-SCR-help men	40s, Lucca	f/b, 9	home
Sofia	trustee	SCR	60s, N. Italy	f/b, 20s	home
Nora	trustee	F-help men	70s, Chgo	f/b	retired bkkpr
President	president	F	50s, Chgo	English only	home
Lorena	financial sec	no position	60s, Lucca	b/Eng weak, 20s	retired factory
Masie	entertainment	no position	60s, Chgo	b/Ital weak	waitress
Gloria	recording sec	F	50s, Chgo	f/b	teacher
Jeanne	1st v-p	F	50s, Wisc	English only	home

F = feminist
SCR = peasant indirection/Susan Carol Rogers
why? = why bother to discuss?
do it right = negotiate equitably
help men = subservience to men

f/b = fully bilingual
b/Eng weak = Ital dominant
b/Ital weak = Eng dominant
number = age at immigration

[1] Note that some women vacillate from one philosophical position to another.

working: one in a doctor's office, one as a waitress, one as a teacher. Two of the older women have retired, one from a book-keeper's job, the other from a factory job of long standing. The remaining four stopped working as soon as they had children and have continued to stay at home; two provide services in their husbands' businesses, but they would probably categorize themselves as traditional wives and mothers.

These women can be considered inner core members since they are either officers or trustees. Several are also members of the outer core, remaining powerful influencers of opinion, regardless of whether or not they are current members of the administration. All, except for the president, the first vice-president, and me, are members of fifteen or twenty years standing. They have held myriad offices, chaired important events, played bocce, decorated, cleaned, and performed the thousands of functions which the Collandia Ladies' Club yearly takes upon itself. They present themselves, therefore, as a formidable force of actors whose current routine is to verify that money has been allocated in such a way that the yearly books can be closed to the satisfaction of all concerned. This routine is not new, for there is a tradition that the Ladies' Club meets with the Men's Club president at the beginning of each fiscal year to finalize expenses. Not new, either, is the tension located in gender which always arises about what, specifically, the ladies owe the men.

The *message form* is colloquial English with occasional code-switching to Italian. Much of the nitty-gritty of the exchange, the *message content* about who owes what, occurs between Rina and Ciro so that they fall into an *act sequence* of rhythmic exchange that moves to a quicker, louder pace ultimately leading to what I call a rupture. At this point there is sudden silence. Much overlapping, some of it unintelligible, goes on throughout except for during these ruptures. Sometimes side conversations can also be heard.

The components called *rules for interaction* are defined by Saville-Troike as "prescriptive statements of behavior, of how people 'should' act, which are tied to the shared values of the speech community" (147). Typical examples include "turn-taking rules in conversation" (147). In this instance, however, these *rules for in-*

teraction define what topics the women are allowed to discuss publicly with the Men's Club president. That is, there are to be no complaints by the women about whether or not it is correct to follow the bylaws, which prescribe that only $1,000 may be kept in the Ladies' Club treasury. Rather, what should be discussed is how the bylaws are being followed. This means that the burden of explaining the figures in their books remains with the Ladies' Club treasurer Rina, who should do most of the talking to Ciro. Any public entreaty she makes to lessen the financial responsibility of the Ladies' Club can be accepted or denied by him, since he is in full agreement that the purpose of the Ladies' Club is to help the men. He is also eager for the money because, in the midst of refurbishing the banquet room and the kitchen, he has bills to pay. For the most part, since he is the one who is entitled to authority, he can say anything he wants.

The *norms of interpretation* concern the following of the real rules of the Collandia Club which involve working hard to make money, being frugal, accepting what you are entitled to and nothing more, following tradition. Because these real rules adhere to oral traditions, reconstructions of them depend upon the memories of those who were present at an earlier time. Therefore, much of the conversation between the women specifies who has always done and/or paid for what. In addition, much discussion has to do with enculturating those who are less in-the-know into these long-standing traditions.

Stubbs says, "Transcribing conversation into the visual medium is a useful estrangement device, which can show up complex aspects of conversational coherence which pass us by as real-time conversationalists or observers" (20). I propose to use the estrangement device of discourse analysis to look at gender notions of power and powerlessness as encoded in language. Here I use a feminist frame of reference which takes as (historically) important the things men do. In it men operate as the default category and women operate as other. I shall show how in their discourse these Collandia women re-create the man-as-powerful and woman-as-powerless themes with which they are societally familiar. Power in this case has to do with money, with who controls the purse strings of their auxiliary. I shall also show how their language is imbedded in a microcosm of strategies, mostly of indirection, which historically have been used by the powerless against the powerful. Actually, this is my point—that the participants in this discourse are not fully aware of the deeper implications of gender roles and *bella figura*, the cultural code, which constrain them to act in the ways that they do. In point of fact, this transcript shows them bringing the two together in an almost seamless way. For, as Goffman says, "we all act better than we know how" (74).

This meeting is ostensibly about money, but money is really a moot point because profits beyond $1,000 go to the men anyway. So what is the meeting really about? I think that one thing it is about concerns the tensions involved in maintaining *bella figura* in the handling of this money. That is, the Collandia Ladies' Club accepts that the predominant club is the Collandia Men's Club, but they want acknowledgment for themselves. Not just for their part in making this club work, but for their organized, rule-bound, tradition-following part in making this club work. Scott calls this kind of discourse a hidden transcript of resistance, a "creation of autonomous social space for assertion of dignity" (198). In other words, the Collandia Ladies' Club wants acknowledgment of their *bella figura*.

Different women see this issue differently. Jeanne, who is not Italian at all—only married to a second generation Italian—adopts the most direct method of negotiating with Ciro, the Men's Club president. (On the transcript I have marked her comments "*#1 direct.*") For her the issue is clear-cut; "They're going to get it, anyway," but it has to do with the "principle" in "our books." Jeanne expects that saying what she means will accomplish what she wants—that Ciro will reimburse her for expenses that are rightly his, that monies used by the women will be shown by the women as their expenses, that the logic and justice of her method will be recognized by all. As an American-born feminist, for her the most important issue has to do with equality of representation. She is involved in establishing her role in the discourse of power but she fails to understand *bella figura*. So when she says, "see?" to the others to indicate Ciro's compliance and fairness, she is the only one to view the matter as closed.

On the other hand, Rina, an Italian who came here at age 12, engages in almost total indirection. (I have marked her comments "*#2 powerless.*" They form part of the prologue.) She looks for solidarity: "Pretty soon he's going to come—you're all here. You're all officers. Ask him to deduct . . ." When Nora code-switches to Italian and asks her why she has to pay for events where the Ladies' Club didn't take in the profits, she answers, "Well, we gotta. That's why we're here." Rina speaks what would seem to be the quintessential language of the powerless: We are here to fulfill an agenda that we don't really control. While establishing this conflict, however, in some ways, she also seems to be reciting lines to a script. Note especially the rhythmically balanced way she sets up her initial exchange of appositives with Ciro: "of all the money," "everything that we collected," "all the profits," "the money that we have," "how it all was spent." The language and prosody here are similar to classical dramatic exposition in which the conflict is briefly encapsulated for the audience at the beginning of Act One. It seems fair to say that, upon closer examination, there is more (unconsciously?) going on in Rina's discourse than meets the eye.

In fact, THE PROLOGUE can be regarded as a contest between the language of the powerless and the "direct" language of power, all spoken with no man present:

THE PROLOGUE (no man present)

Rina:	Pretty soon Ciro's going to come—
#2 powerless	you're all here. You're all officers.
	Ask him to deduct this $826.95.
	It's all their expenses . . .
	Easter, Mother's Day, Xmas decorations . . .

[overlapping comments]

Jeanne:	But wait, you owe them for the dinner yet.
#1 direct	Deduct that 800 . . .

Rina: You, you deduct.
#2 powerless

Frida: That's right.
echo #1 direct with
no man present

Rina: You deduct.
#2 powerless   See if they're willing to do it.
                         If they're willing to deduct, you do it.

Jeanne: That's right.
#1 direct

Sofia: Why not?
echo #1 direct with
no man present

Jeanne: It comes down to a matter of
#1 direct   you guys are letting them do it to you.

Sofia: That's right.
echo #1 direct with
no man present

Jeanne: They're going to get it anyway,
#1 direct   but to me it's the principle.
                         If they want to put these women down,
                         I mean let's . .

None of this is performative language, none of it public—the
women are simply discussing among themselves what they should
do before their dialogue with the Men's Club President.

   When Ciro, an Italian who immigrated at 17, appears, the action becomes almost like a play with the women as the chorus and
Ciro as the main actor. (This section is marked "ACT ONE, The
Show.") Here is the Don with his handmaidens metaphorically
kissing his hand. In the opening lines Rina has set the stage for her
entreaty: "Whenever you have a moment, we're ready. We want
to show you our books. We want to pay the bills." She will now

take the main role opposite Ciro, and the rest of the women, unconsciously perhaps, will drift back and forth between performance and audience, but all—except Jeanne—are privy to the
show.

Sofia too has entered into the play by code-switching into
diminuitives. "*Cirino*" she calls him, perhaps to mimic a sort of
tongue-in-cheek playfulness which she sees as appropriate to the
unfolding drama in which he must be cajoled. This mood contrasts with her "why not?/that's right" refrain, which has been
dead serious throughout the earlier transcript. She has also called
the women "so soft." However, that was the discourse of power,
appropriate, she seems to think, when only the ladies are present.
That this language is a departure for Sofia is evidenced by the fact
that the president remarks on her sweetness, "Did you hear how
nice Sofia's saying, 'Sit down, Honey?'"

Throughout "ACT ONE, THE SHOW," there is a rhythm
established which indicates the performance of a metaphorical
song and dance. For example, Ciro reiterates "yeah" three times as
Rina dances around him with a recitation of the financial items to
be discussed. (Notice the circles I have used around "yeah.") They
almost seem to indicate that Ciro, too, is circling, waiting for the
request he knows is about to come. Rina uses seven synonyms as
a sort of introductory refrain: "money," "everything," "collected,"
"profits," "money," "outstanding," "spent." (These words I have
boxed off.) The first comment Ciro makes before walking off—
"where's my money?"—reiterates the refrain Rina has begun.
"Wait," she says, postponing an answer to his question. It is as if
he has disturbed her rhythmic incantation of what he owes her:
"*questi qui*," "*questi qui*," "spent at Easter," "Easter eggs," "Easter
bunny," "Mother's Day," "the presidential banquet." These are her
"lines," so to speak. (I have underlined them twice and marked
them "incantation.")

Rina:	Of all the [money] that was passed to us	[ ] =
	from last year,	*synonyms*
	all the . . . [everything] that we [collected] . . .	*as refrain*
	all the [profits] that we made . . .	*for entreaty*

Ciro: (Yeah) . .

Rina: The |money| that we have |outstanding| . . .
                   it or how it all was |spent| . . .

Ciro: (Yeah) where's my money?

Rina: Wait.

[laughter]

Rina: *Ora questi qui, questi qui,*   ═══════ =
                   (now these here, these here)   *items men*
                   they were sp<u>ent</u> like at Easter, *should pay for*
                   E<u>aster eggs</u> . . .   *—incantation*

Ciro: (Yeah) . . .

Rina: E<u>aster bun</u>ny and then for <u>Mother</u>'s Day
                   and the presid<u>ential</u> banquet . . .
                   so the ladies feel that this . . .

   Finally, she gets to the point, which is that "the ladies feel"
that they have been shortchanged. (Notice her use of "feel",
which implies a sort of web-like intuition. Jeanne had said, "Do
you know what I'm saying?" more of an intellectualization.)
"They want to take it off the money that we owe you for the
Xmas party," she states bluntly. It is her first direct statement.
Hearing her request, Ciro becomes angry. He cries, "*Porca miseria*"— glossed to "for crying out loud"—an expression of annoy-
ance, and intentionally walks off. And so this act comes to an
abrupt and dramatic close. (Here I have written "*rupture.*")

Rina: so the ladies feel that this . . .

[Many unintelligible comments]

Rina: They want to take it off the money
#1 direct   that we owe you for the Xmas party.
(first time)

Ciro: (walks off)   *Porca miseria!*   **rupture**
                    (For crying out loud!)

The attention is clearly on Ciro now. In fact, his performance is so terribly important—anticlimactic perhaps?—that we all comment on it.

In this interlude we become audience to Ciro, for his departure has brought the song and dance to a close. Rina, who had briefly tried a somewhat direct approach to set up her plea, drops this rhetorical strategy. She says, "See, I mean, why do we want to get aggravated?" In this plea she replicates the age-old powerlessness of women theme, the role of accepting subservience. Italian-born Sofia drops the playfulness of before and speaks directly, "Come over here, Ciro." I attempt a Jeanne-like logic which, despite itself, does not fail to take into account the drama Ciro has invoked. "He's coming back," I say, implying that we get another chance at the dialogue. Is this an aside? Do I sense that we haven't yet finished the play? Only Jeanne remains silent. Has she not remarked it as an "exit"? (See "*INTERLUDE*" and "*rupture commented on.*")

[confusion]

Sofia: Come over here, Ciro, Ciro . . .

Rina: See, I mean
                    why do we want to get aggravated?

[many comments]

Gloria: No, he's coming back.
                    He's going to go to the bathroom.
Rina: No, he's going to go. . .

When Ciro returns, ACT TWO begins. Jeanne again approaches him with the direct and logical discourse of the American feminist. She knows that "we have to give it [the money] up anyway," but she is still concerned with the principle she mentioned earlier. "Normally," she says, the men pay for the stamps used on their mailings. She implies that she does not think that his response will be anything other than normal, almost as if she has not seen him yell *"Porca miseria"* and run off. At the end of her prose-like dialogue with him—notice that there are few rhythmic breath groups of phrases, and no repetitions—she is content that they have reached consensus about paying for the New Year's Eve mailing, so she says, "There-see?" to Rina, meaning that everything is now settled. (I have again marked her comments "*#1 direct*.")

Jeanne: *#1 direct*	No, the men— it comes down to a matter of principle . . .
Ciro:	Ok.
Jeanne: *#1 direct*	We have to give it up anyway, but we want to be reimbursed by you so that our books reflect what we've really done. Do you know what I'm saying? When we send out your cenettas, you should be paying for those stamps. Normally they do.

[Nora chimes in approval.]

Ciro:	We do. We pay for those cenettas.
Rina:	But like I sent out New Year's Eve. I sent out New Year's Eve. Nobody reimbursed us for that.
Ciro:	If you sent out New Year's Eve, you got the bill, we pay you for New Year's Eve.

song and dance

Jeanne: *#1 direct*	There—see?

Rina, however, is unwilling to "settle" yet. Earlier, she had begun with Ciro the same sort of repartee as in Act One: "New Year's Eve" is rhythmically invoked twice by both of them, but for different purposes. (I have boxed off their comments.) She means it as an example of how she has been overlooked by the Men's Club; he means it as an example of their willingness to be equitable. It is a repetition of the song and dance of Act One, which Ciro had brought to such an abrupt close.

Now when Jeanne says, "There-see?", Rina launches her final—and most important—performance. (I have marked this the "final performance.") She says, "Oh, well, I don't HAVE the BILL," with great emphasis on both "HAVE" and "BILL," thereby contesting Jeanne's direct "settling" of the account. Ciro, too, has been involved in the settling of the account by agreeing to the "bill" as proof of sale. We can look at this indignant comment of Rina's two ways. Either she is implying that "having the bill" is not necessary for someone of her moral fiber, the treasurer who would never attempt to get reimbursed for an illegitimate expense. Or, because she knows that she has the canceled check from the E.P. Post Office which is better than having the bill, she is setting Ciro up for a fall. Whatever she means—and I suggest that she is (subconsciously) out to ensnare Ciro—she effectively re-starts the argument.

Rina: Oh, well,   ↑ } *final perfor-*
                 I don't HAVE the (BILL)   } *mance*
                 (LOUDER TONE, HIGHER PITCH)   } *re-starts argument*

Next she asks a (seemingly) innocent question, "Who bought the stamps?" to which she already has the answer. Ciro speaks from a position of power. "Maybe we bought the stamps," he says. Again, they engage in a song and dance in which each takes a turn repeating the significant words of the other: "stamps," "who bought the stamps," "check," and "money." (I have circled these money words and put boxes around "stamps.") Ostensible powerlessness (indirection) seems to be the position that Rina is most comfortable with, because she is able to react against it in a wonderfully dramatic scene.

                 I-I-I gave her the CHECK—
                 how could you—

WHAT YOU SAYING—
THAT SHE GETS THE
MONEY TWICE?

 powerful
starring
moment

She shouts in indignation. It is her starring moment. In it she up-stages Ciro.

Rina: (overlapping) Well, who bought the stamps?   **entrapment**
                                                          (indirect)

Frida: Excuse me . . . I know that Norma
              . . . (unintelligible)

Rina: (overlap) Whoever bought the stamps . . .

Ciro: Well, who bought the stamps?
              Maybe we bought the stamps!

Rina: No, no, no!

Ciro: How do you know?
              if we don't know who bought the stamps . . .

Rina: Because I have them all in here   **invoking of**
              from the—   **authority**
              They were bought—
              they were bought from the E. Postmaster
              E. P. Postmaster
              I have the check!

Ciro: (continuing and overlapping) because . . .

Gloria: (overlapping and correcting) E. P. she's saying

Rina: E. P. . . .

Pres: Oh, Matilda!

several voices: Matilda B!

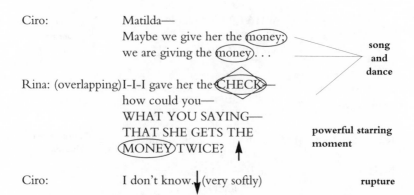

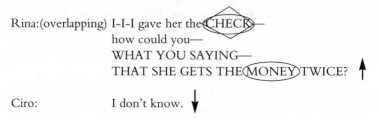

Another RUPTURE occurs. Ciro's ending comment of "I don't know" is spoken softly, no longer a part of the tempo previously established. Unlike his metrical "we give her the money/we are giving the money," it is now clear that Rina has outperformed him. He knows it, she knows it, and so do all the women who have been part of the chorus. Only Jeanne, perhaps, oblivious to the subtleties of the discourse, does not.

Tannen says, "Cultural patterns . . . . provide a range from which individuals choose strategies that they habitually use in expressing their individual styles" (*Talking Voices* 80). My explanation of Rina's style is that she has created the strategy of "*sprezzatura*" or "studied carelessness," a term recommended by Castiglione in *The Courtier*. Her repetitions of "You—you deduct" and "I sent out New Year's Eve" and "who bought the stamps?" imply a lack of entitlement for the Ladies' Club even though she knows better. Despite the fact that she is legitimately in the right, she chooses not to make her claims outright to Ciro. After all, she could have said, "I don't have the bill. I have the cancelled check for the stamps." But she deliberately withholds this information until later. When she finally does tell him, she invokes the authority of "Postmaster" and "check" two times— Ciro never mentions these words.

Perhaps she senses that she needs a moment of highly emotional display, a *figura* of sorts, in order to have him realize the legitimacy of what she has to say. For whenever the argument appears to be settled, she brings it up again. The first rupture—his yelling out of *"Porca miseria"*—occurs because Ciro is in control; the second rupture—when he almost whispers "I don't know"— occurs because he is not. At the end, if Ciro answers "no" to "What you saying . . . . that she gets the money twice?" he admits Rina was right; if he says "yes," he makes himself look stupid. So he has no viable answer. Therefore, Rina's performance, embedded in the context of (seemingly) powerless female discourse, has invoked the all-important cultural construct of *bella figura* by putting Ciro in the position of making a *brutta figura* no matter what answer he gives. By saying "I don't know" he admits that she has won the challenge. The power of the performance is hers—there are no words left for him.

All of us on the transcript, except possibly Jeanne, are, in some sense, engaged in carrying on a role in this play. I am being initiated into the discourse by Nora, who is describing the unresolved tensions that have existed at the Collandia for some time. Sofia is pretending to believe in male dominance with Ciro and acting directly powerful with the women. Ciro himself is acting like the Men's Club President. The other women mostly pr' vide the choral backdrop. But Rina's role is the most directly performed of all because, in her attempt to impose her views upon Ciro, she is most in need of drama. Thus, she chooses to perform *bella figura*, a juxtapositioning of cultural forms, which she is able to invoke because she is both bilingual and bicultural.

But Ciro is bilingual and bicultural, too. I maintain that he knows exactly what she is doing, and—perhaps even admires and approves. It is interesting to note that at the end of the tape the two of them get down to the business of settling the bills amicably and with dispatch. "Come on, Ciro," Rina says, "we've gotta take care of this." She sits down. He sits down. The bills get paid with very little drama. Rina has won, so to speak, her right to deduct. Silverman says that the task of Colleverde women is "to see to the public display of the household's collective identity," so to some extent Ciro has a stake in what Rina does, especially if we view the Collandia Club as a extension of family in the New World (*Three Bells of Civilization* 206). That is, as an Italian he has an unconscious understanding and appreciation of Rina's strategies because they are not unfamiliar to him. So he acquiesces in applauding her performance, and they are able to move on to the business at hand.

To return to my initial questions:

What is the social context of this interaction? That is, how do these women present themselves? How are they members of the same speech community?

The social context is that all the women are members of the Collandia Ladies' Club who know the real rules and are familiar with the issue of entitlement, the topic of almost all their overt discussions. This entitlement obtains both among the women themselves and between the women and the men. Moreover, their familiarity with the code of *bella figura* gives them a shared knowledge of rules both for their own conduct—for how they present themselves—and for their interpretation of each other's speech.

They show this knowledge by attempting to get Ciro to return after the first *rupture*, after he has shown the necessary pizzazz to win the first round. They need to engage with him again in order to make their entreaty work. At the second *rupture*, however, they realize that the *tour de force* has been Rina's, and they say nothing, knowing that there is nothing to say. She has won.

What are the communicative strategies at work here? How do they create conversational involvement?

The overlapping, the frequently poetic-like repetition, the pace of what could be called a "high-involvement" style, are what Tannen considers "ethnic style," as are Rina's (and Sofia's) strategies of indirection. "Conversational involvement" in the drama

comes from all the participants' realization that a *bella figura* performance has occurred. Thus, except for Jeanne, they are speaking
in English but performing in Italian, a sort of cultural transference
of one group of rules to another. Therefore, as insiders clearly separate from outsiders, they are able to weave for themselves an
emotional and philosophical involvement that operates throughout their conversation with Ciro.

Where does performance occur? How is this an example of a
performance which is communally constituted?

Performance occurs twice; both times between Rina and Ciro
as they battle each other for control of the finances; both end
in what I have marked as *rupture*. In the first case, we know
that Rina is starting a performance because she begins a rhythmic
intonation of synonyms and lists of items for which the Men's
Club bears responsibility. She speaks in breath groups of threes,
frequently repeating herself, using repetition for what Tannen calls
"the central linguistic meaning-making strategy" (*Talking Voices*
97) of poetics. Except for the one time she directly asks Ciro for
what she wants, Rina engages largely in indirect language, also a
poetic strategy. But her performance does not work because Ciro
abruptly walks off without giving her an answer.

The second time Rina signals her performance with a change
in stress, pitch, and duration. Again she speaks in breath groups of
three lines; again she employs repetition to create a poetic paral-
lelism that becomes more and more authoritative as it escalates. The
diction she chooses in her repetitions invokes an official financial
authority: stamps, Postmaster, check. At the end, her voice becomes the loudest it ever has been on the tape. She also uses a pause
right before the coup de grace, "that she gets the money twice?", as
a signal to pay attention. This time her performance works because
Ciro is cowed. All he can do is mumble softly, "I don't know."

We know when the performances have ended because, in
both cases, the normal give and take of conversation ends. The
first time entails a confusion of overlapping comments where all
the women become an audience to Ciro's dramatic exit; the second time, the silence signals Ciro's and the audience's acknowl-
edgement of his defeat. Bauman says, "A not insignificant part of

the capacity of performance to transform social structure . . . re-
sides in the power that the performer derives from the control
over his audience afforded him by the formal appeal of his performance" (*Verbal Art* 16). In this case, "control" means the power to
stop what had been proceeding conversationally. In other words,
Rina achieves power because her audience is stopped in its tracks
by her cleverness.

The ladies have helped constitute this performance by their
willingness to let Rina speak for them, a willingness to be the audience which is heard in their back-channel hums of approval
throughout the discourse. Rina, too, is clearly considering their
participation, and speaking for them, as she states in her entreaty:
"You're all here, you're all officers, ask him to deduct." During
her second performance, their mention of Matilda as the woman
who bought the stamps lends credibility to her outrage at Ciro for
implying that he gave her the money.

What role does indirection and the view of women as powerless users of language play in this discourse? Stubbs maintains that
much of language use is indirect and that "a central problem for
analysis is therefore the depth of indirection involved" (147). This
insight allows us to view much of the discourse in the transcript as
meaning something other than what it literally is saying. For example, Rina's "We want to show you our books. We want to pay
the bills" probably really means, "We want you to acknowledge
that some of what we have paid was not really our responsibility."
But because her meaning is expressed ambiguously, if she happens
to be wrong, she can save face later by claiming that she really
wanted simply to "show our books." This is the power of indirection: paradoxically, it can claim powerlessness for itself and so not
be left without any way to repair a *brutta figura*.

Geertz says that culture reveals itself in particulars of time and
place, so the overarching question—again—of this analysis remains: How are language and culture inextricably bound? I answer that discourse analysis serves as an important tool in
describing this bond, for it shows us how one creates and, at the
same time, is created by the other. That is, to examine the language of this transcript without acknowledging the primacy of the

cultural construct of *bella figura* as a frame is virtually impossible. Otherwise, much of what goes on becomes unclear, or worse— nonsensical. But we also cannot understand *bella figura* as a cultural construct unless it is played out as a specific linguistic performance. Otherwise, there is no meaning in what occurs. They are two sides of the same coin. That is, if we do not understand the intense importance of display and spectacle in this speech community, we also fail to realize how Rina's artful performance operates in the claiming of power. And if we do not understand how Rina's artful performance operates in the claiming of power, we also fail to realize the intense importance of display and spectacle in this speech community.

In conclusion, these women's ways of speaking, both gendered and cultured, are dependent upon the context of the Collandia Ladies' Club for their full meaning. This transcript, a wonderfully rich and woven tapestry, allows us to understand that *bella figura* operates in language as well as in behavior. Rina's performance, a dazzling display of verbal art, validates yet again the cultural code in which it is embedded.

Conclusion

The preceding study has broken ground in many ways. First of all, it focuses on a group never studied before, a club of immigrant women who came to Chicago (largely) from Lucca after World War II. It also deconstructs a metaphor heretofore never studied: the Italian cultural construct called *fare bella figura*. In defining and contextualizing this concept, it explores the ways in which language and behavior are inextricably bound—some would even say created—by *bella figura*. In order to emphasize the underlying Italian mores of the Collandia, I deliberately reject "Italian American" and use "Italian" instead.

My study is polyhedral; its conceptual framework combines Goffman and Bourdieu, the performance studies of Briggs and Bauman, and principles of discourse analysis from Gumperz and Stubbs. My methodology, always feminist in point of view, is ethnographic: I have written a "thick description" of the Collandia Ladies' Club. Of necessity, this description incorporates an analysis of women's language, a documentation of women's roles in immigration, an exploration of the social power that lies in performing *bella figura* well. Above all, perhaps, mine is a study of identity.

This identity hinges upon the solidarity which my ladies derive from defining, redefining, and upholding their own realities within the Collandia. To these women whose lives revolve around families and homes, the notion of club is especially important, for it provides them with what Goffman would call their stage. Here, unfettered by other demands, they freely construct roles of power for themselves. For the most part, they have been onlookers in the public arena. They have watched their husbands achieve the Great American Dream. Their children have become Americans, their grandchildren even more so. But the Collandia is theirs. As they play out the performances that separate the insiders from the outsiders, their roles allow them recognition in their own right.

Farr documents how Mexican immigrant women "create and recreate their culture, over the generations, through what has been called verbal art" (3). Similarly, I see *bella figura* as the cultural code which the Collandia Ladies validate over and over through their performance of it.

What are some of the implications for a continuation of this work? Women's clubs present an important area for further research, for they serve as bridges between public and private domains. Seemingly quasi-public forums, in reality clubs frequently operate more like families, offering supportive environments for women who may be silenced elsewhere. For example, at the Collandia, indirection is not necessarily manipulative nor is powerful language necessarily direct. Examining language use in this "community of practice" allows us to revise our notions of women as powerless users of language. My revision of female language use might enable us to document other strategies of solidarity and strength. An examination of the Collandia also helps to dispel the myth that identity is uniform and monolithic, showing instead a bilingual/ bicultural continuum with ever-changing performances. Sometimes these tend more towards the Italian end of the spectrum, sometimes not.

My research also shows that support of cultural diversity (academia's and business's current buzzword) may be infinitely more complicated than it seems. After all, these Collandia ladies, whose ways with words are sometimes such a puzzlement, are Euro-Americans, part of the white community usually thought of as mainstream. If cross-cultural misunderstandings can occur with them, how many other unwarranted assumptions might we be making in our dealings with other groups who also do not seem particularly different? Postmodern ideology tells us that language does not provide "an unproblematic access to reality" (Faigley 8). This has, in fact, been one of my major points. Accordingly, more research among other white ethnic groups might be profitable in pointing out how to avoid potential dissonance in communication.

I also think that Italian Americans can be linked culturally to the Italians from whom they have descended. Conventional wisdom says that the longer people stay in a country, the more they become like the natives. We used to characterize the American immigrant experience, in fact, as a melting pot. But this is a naive view of culture as static and only surface stuff. Could it be that this unfortunate metaphor has led to the years of silence documented by Helen Barolini in her discussion of why so few Italian American women have become writers? Could an emphasis upon the culture of *bella figura* alleviate the literary inferiority these women have perhaps felt and empower them to write? If so, all of American literature (and the Academy as well, in which Italian American women are also underrepresented) could be the richer for their experiences.

Surely, realizing the importance of *bella figura* allows us to read differently Italian American texts, including films. For example, to view performance as a cultural imperative deepens our understanding of *Big Night*: the brothers' failure occurs when Louie Prima never attends their feast, thus precluding their *bella figura*. In *True Love*, the specter of *brutta figura* explains the depths of Donna's humiliation if she doesn't marry Michael. Other observations could be made for other works.[1]

One Final Thought

Close to the end of my research, my son Gian Carlo came upon a book which serves as a fitting final comment. *Feminine Feminists: Cultural Practices in Italy*, edited by Giovanna Miceli Jeffries, articulates a phenomenon largely unknown to American feminists: the process of *affidamento* (entrustment) espoused by Diotima, a leading feminist community in Verona, which defines the Italian understanding of feminism.[2] In the *affidamento*

> younger and inexperienced women entrust themselves to other, older, more powerful and influential women. These women mentors become the younger women's mediators to the outside world, thus allowing the estab-

lishment of a feminine order of thought and practice.[3]
(*Feminine Feminists* xiii–iv)

The importance of this find lies in its differing view of empower-
ment, which I will contextualize specifically within the framework of the Collandia Ladies' Club.

As an American feminist, I am interested in power. In fact, I
paid endless attention to the ramifications of power in all the operations of the Collandia Club. Frequently my single-minded interest in it led me to fear that I was not analyzing my field notes in
a sufficiently emic manner, for the word power itself never was
mentioned once by any of my native informants. Occasionally,
Toni told me that one particular member or other liked to be *considerata*, which I translated as "considered" meaning "paid attention to." Slowly, it dawned on me that there was something about
her use of the word that I was not understanding. Toni seemed to
invoke it as a sort of warning about appropriate behavior on my
part, for she would then urge me to make a particular effort
to telephone that member to seek her accord on the issue in
question.

Finally, I looked up "*considerata.*" *Il Nuovo Zingarelli* listed, as a
seventh definition of *considerare*: "*stimare, avere in pregio; in quell'am-
biente non é considerato*" ("esteem, hold in prestige; in that setting he
is not held in high regard"). There it was—the link between
power and *figura* that I had intuited. Toni was telling me that I
needed to allow Collandia ladies the power of a *bella figura*. She
was telling me indirectly, of course, and urging me to deal with
them indirectly, too. And in so doing, Toni was empowering me;
in effect "activat[ing] a vertical hierarchy within the women's
community . . . express[ing her]self with its own language, culture, and ethical standards," (*Feminine Feminism* xiv) precisely
through the *affidamento* described above. She was drawing together the discourses of feminism and *bella figura* in a uniquely Italian way. Through her use of words, she was showing me how to
be an insider.

But words are words, after all, some might say, not the sticks
and stones that make up real power. On the contrary, I might an-

swer, echoing Toni Morrison: our lives take on the shape of the stories we tell. They, too, can break our bones. So words—and our abilities to present ourselves, which frequently depend upon words—may provide a direct link to our sense of ourselves, to our sense of our own significance.

Words, for example, are the building blocks of this book. What is its overall significance?

First of all, in telling stories that have not been told before, it shows that there is not just one Italian American experience. There are many. The lives of these Collandia Club women represent one of them. Furthermore, as they take charge of their own spheres, my Collandia women are redefining a mysterious and multifaceted process which we call Americanization. Ironically, this Americanization involves retaining their *bella figura*, and so their Italian-ness. Here, where membership in the Club is a way of being Italian, ethnicity is more than symbolic—it is a way to belong. In the same way that *bella figura* is central to Italian culture, other cultures may well have other constructs which unlock their identities. Readers may find it useful to explore their own.

For me, this tale has been a tale of transformation, a deepening of my own Italian roots.[4] Sometimes I waxed analytical and professorial, creating a sort of macroethnography in the "Real Rules of the Club," which described emically the true workings of *bella figura* throughout all its events. Sometimes I waxed confessional and personal, deconstructing for the audience (and for myself) how I had been drawn into both *bella figura* and the language of indirection frequently employed by the Collandia Ladies. In my combination of emic and etic perspectives, I created a multilayered view of the identity of this community, an identity both infused and circumscribed with the performance of *bella figura*.

More and more I became dazzled by the power such performance exerts in the enrichment of ordinary human events: the staging of a fashion show, the ritual negotiation of club funds, the research and writing of books such as this. And *bella figura* became not only the subject of my study but the magic that effected my transformation. *Bella* indeed marks this approach that infuses the real with the beauty and harmony of studied nonchalance. More

than that, *figura* dramatizes throughout life's many ordinary moments an ideal which we intuit and feel when it is staged for us.
Indeed, humans have always known that dramatic performance
involves the kind of magic that can transform.

In their ability to dramatize much of life, my Collandia Ladies
have created a richness which speaks to the power of the human
spirit. Their gift to me is this lesson: I live my life, not only according to their cultural construct—which is my heritage, too—
but with conscious appreciation of how it civilizes that life. And I
believe that if we, the human race, intend to enhance our civilization, perhaps it is incumbent upon us to always and everywhere
fare bella figura.

Appendix A

Transcript of Financial Meeting

Sentences are broken spatially into breath groups. Caps imply that tone is louder and pitch higher.

THE PROLOGUE (no man present)

Rina:
#2 powerless

Pretty soon Ciro's going to come—
you're all here. You're all officers.
Ask him to deduct this $826.95.
It's all their expenses. . .
Easter, Mother's Day, Xmas decorations . . .

[overlapping comments]

Jeanne:
#1 direct

But wait, you owe them for the dinner yet.
Deduct that 800. . . .

Rina:
#2 powerless

You, you deduct.

Frida:
echo #1 direct with
no man present

That's right.

Rina:
#2 powerless

You deduct.
See if they're willing to do it.
If they're willing to deduct, you do it.

Jeanne:
#1 direct

That's right.

Sofia:
echo #1 direct with
no man present

Why not?

Jeanne:
#1 direct

It comes down to a matter of principle . . .
you guys are letting them do it to you.

Sofia:
echo #1 direct with
no man present

That's right.

Jeanne:
#1 direct

They're going to get it anyway,
but to me it's the principle.
If they want to put these women down,
I mean let's . . .

ACT ONE, The Show

"Hi, Ciro" from many as Men's President walks in.

Rina:

Whenever you have a moment, eh . . .

Sofia: (in baby voice)

Sit down, Cirino.
Metteti al tavolo, Ciro.
(Sit at the table, little Ciro.)

Rina:

Whenever you have a moment, we're ready.
We want to show you our books.
We want to pay the bills.

[Additional comments unintelligible. Ciro briefly goes elsewhere.]

PROLOGUE (continued)

Nora (switching to Italian and addressing Rina):
language of power . . .

Questa roba che l'hai scritta te,
l'hai fatti te i soldi di quelle lì?
Allora perché devi pagà'?
(This stuff that you wrote down,

language of power, no man present

did you make the money from it?
Then why do you have to pay?)

Rina:
#2 powerless

Well, we gotta.
That's why we're here.

Sofia:
language of power with no man present

That's because they find the women so soft.

ACT ONE (continued)

[Ciro returns.]

Sofia: Sit down, Ciro.

Pres: Did you hear how nice Sofia's saying,
           "Sit down, Honey?"

[Overlapping comments—much back channel "uhhm" as approval throughout following section]

Rina: Of all the money that was passed to us
           from last year,
           all the . . . everything that we collected . . .
           all the profits that we made . . .

           [box] = *synonyms as refrain for entreaty*

Ciro: Yeah ...

Rina: The money that we have outstanding ...
             it or how it all was spent ...

Ciro: Yeah, where's my money?

Rina: Wait.

[laughter]

Rina: *Ora questi qui, questi qui,*
             (now these here, these here)
             they were spent like at Easter,
             Easter eggs ....

Ciro: Yeah ...

Rina: Easter bunny and then for Mother's Day
             and the presidential banquet ...
             so the ladies feel that this ...

[Many unintelligible comments]

Rina: They want to take it off the money
#1 direct   that we owe you for the Xmas party.
(first time)

◯ = *rhythmic*
      repetition

‖ = *items men should pay for*
—incantation

Ciro: (walks off)   *Porca miseria!*

(For crying out loud!)

INTERLUDE

[confusion]

Sofia: Come over here, Ciro, Ciro . . .

Rina: See, I mean
why do we want to get aggravated?

[Many comments]

Gloria: No, he's coming back.
He's going to go to the bathroom.

Rina: No, he's going to go . . .

ACT TWO

[Ciro returns.]

Jeanne: No, the men— it comes down to a matter of
#1 *direct*   principle . . . .

Ciro: Ok.

Jeanne: We have to give it up anyway,
#1 direct   but we want to be reimbursed by you
            so that our books reflect what we've really done.
            Do you know what I'm saying?
            When we send out your cenettas,
            you should be paying for those stamps.
            Normally they do.

[Nora chimes in approval.]

Ciro: We do. We pay for those cenettas.
Rina: But like— I sent out New Year's Eve.
            I sent out New Year's Eve.
            Nobody reimbursed us for that.

Ciro: If you sent out New Year's Eve,
            you got the bill,
            we pay you for New Year's Eve.

Jeanne: There—see?
#1 direct

Rina: Oh, well,
            I don't HAVE the BILL.
            (LOUDER TONE, HIGHER PITCH)

song and dance

final performance
re-starts argument

Ciro: (continuing)   because everybody come with the bill
                     They say here
                     so many (stamps) for that

[overlapping unintelligible comments]

Rina: Okay here, you know how many members we have;
                     one to every member—
                     We have a hundred and sixty seven.

Ciro: (overlapping) But you gotta . . .

Nora: But they have to have a voucher
                     to put in their books.

Jeanne: Eighty-seven dollars is . . .

Rina: (overlapping) Well, who bought the [stamps?]

Frida: Excuse me . . . I know that Norma
                     . . . (unintelligible)

Rina: (overlap)   Whoever bought the (stamps) . . .

Ciro: Well, who bought the [stamps?]
                     Maybe we bought the [stamps.]

entrapment (indirect)

song and dance

Rina: No, no, no!

Ciro: How do you know?
If we don't know who bought the (stamps) . . .

song and dance (cont.)

= *invoking of authority*

Rina: Because I have them all in here
from the—
They were bought—
they were bought from the E. Postmaster
E.P. Postmaster
I have the (check)

Ciro: (continuing and overlapping) because . . .

Gloria: (overlapping and correcting) E.P. she's saying

Rina: E.P. . . .

Pres: Oh, Matilda!

Several voices: Matilda B!

Ciro: Matilda—
Maybe we give her the (money),
we are giving the (money) . . .

song and dance

Rina: (overlapping)

I-I-I gave her the (CHECK)—
how could you—
WHAT YOU SAYING—
THAT SHE GETS THE (MONEY) TWICE?

} *powerful*
   starring
   moment

Ciro:

I don't know. (very softly) *rupture*

Endnotes

Chapter 1. *A Definition of* Bella Figura

1. Given to me by Umberto Sereni, an Italian History professor at l'universitá di Udine, they are: *Paese Italia, Venti secoli di identitá* written by Ruggiero Romano and published by Donzelli Editore, Roma, in 1994; *Bianco, Rosso e Verde, L'identitá degli italiani*, edited by Giorgio Calcagno, published by Gius. Laterza & Figli, Roma, 1993; and *Stato dell'Italia: Il Bilancio politico, economico, sociale e culturale di un paese che cambia. 180 contributi inediti scritti da piú di 100 specialisti*, edited by Paul Ginsborg, published by Mondadori, 1994. Umberto, aware of my interest in *bella figura*, chose these publications as useful, which makes their lack of the term perhaps even more remarkable.

2. These explanations can be found in any Italian grammar book. I used *L'universo della parola*, written by Fontanesi and Ugolotti, which bills itself as a *corso di educazione linguistica* (linguistic education course) and so devotes itself to greater amounts of descriptive analysis of Italian. In addition, an entire case can be made for the fact that written Italian rhetorical style is often a prime example of *bella figura*. Certainly the language is used in more florid ways than is English. See Kaplan who views divergences in Romance languages in general as more typical than in English, which he represents (rhetorically) as a straight arrow from start to finish.

3. Cf their comments: "Metaphors have entailments through which they highlight and make coherent certain aspects of our experience. A given metaphor may be the only way to highlight and coherently organize exactly those aspects of our experience" (156).

4. I owe to Elliot Judd the realization that it is frequently more important to avoid *brutta figura* than to create a *bella figura* even though the latter gets talked about more. All of my informants agree.

5. While several reputable dictionaries substantiate *cattiva* meaning *meschina* or "miserable" as worse than *brutta* meaning "bad," several of my native *toscani* informants disagreed. They claim that *cattiva figura* is little used, and even if it is used, that there is no difference in meaning between it and *brutta figura*.

6. One of my native informants takes exception to the English

143

word "act" because, she says, one who *fare la figura dello sciocco* is not play-ing at anything but rather truly looking ridiculous. I contend that the use of "play the part of" and "act" are more ambiguous in English, stressing rather outward appearance more than fictitious intent.

7. The implicit issue of social class in this example further under-lines the irony of it. Harwell ended her account of the *mutandine* by saying, "*Aveva sposato un carabiniere.*" ("She had married an Italian gen-darme.") She meant that a *carabiniere* is a man of modest means, whose lifestyle is somehow not consonant with the gift of the expensive panties.

8. Marcia Farr alerted me to this rich literature.

9. Famous Italian American names follow in the same tradition: movie director Francis Ford Coppola, photographer Francesco Scavullo, opera composer GianCarlo Menotti, soprano Anna Moffo, Broadway singer-dancer Bernadette Peters, fashion maven/editor Grace Mirabella.

Chapter 2. *The Conceptual Framework of This Study and Related Literature on Women's Language*

1. Shultz, Florio and Erickson trace this cultural difference to being enculturated in an Italian American speech community in which there exist "multiple audiences and ways of listening as audience mem-bers. . . . [and] multiple conversational floors that speakers could address" (96). Tannen would probably maintain that this Italian American ethnic style is a holdover from the original Italian conversational style.

2. *Colleverde* is a pseudonym for a hilltop village in the province of *Perugia* that operates not unlike the *Lucca* of my informants. Silverman herself defines Central Italy as including the hills and plains of Tuscany where the "characteristic form of settlement outside the major cities was, and is, the community with a nucleated town surrounded by dispersed farms" (*Three Bells of Civilization* x). Silverman's research began in 1960, only slightly later than the period in which my ladies were enculturated.

3. Kohlberg himself found that "women as subjects muddied the findings; they acted as though they were morally 'retarded,' rarely if ever achieving the highest level of moral development" (Bernard 213).

Chapter 3. A History of the Collandia Club

1. Perhaps this agonizingly important desire to eliminate all vestiges of the "Mafia" label with which some Italian Americans concern themselves can, in part, be attributed to its *"brutta figura."*

2. See Joseph LaPalombara's *Democracy Italian Style* for a lucid account of today's Italy, including his explanation of politics as *spettacolo,* that is, what I would call *figura.*

3. The twenty regions are Northern Italy: *Piemonte, Valle d'Aosta, Lombardia, Trentino-Alto Adige, Veneto, Friuli-Venezia Giulia, Liguria, Emilia-Romagna;* Central Italy: *Toscana, Umbria, Marche, Lazio, Abruzzo;* Southern Italy: *Molise, Campania, Puglia, Basilicata, Calabria;* and the islands: *Sicilia* and *Sardegna.*

4. From a geographical point of view—and according to how schoolteachers teach Italian children—Italy is divided into the Northern regions, the Central regions, and the Southern regions plus the two islands of Sicily and Sardinia. (See above.) In common parlance, however, Italy is frequently simply divided into "North" and "South." When these are the only two divisions, generally Rome is the dividing point underneath which Southern Italy begins. But writers, especially American scholars of immigration, have used the terms "Northern" and "Southern" Italian very differently. Covello, for example, in his classic work, *The Social Background of the Italo-American School Child,* calls everything above Naples "Northern" Italy.

According to Sabina Magliocco, *Dopo noi, l'Africa!* is a common Italian saying. ["Underneath us lies Africa."] What is clear is that to be considered "Southern" Italian is to be NOT in the privileged group, however the geography gets figured. See LaPalombara for agreement on this point.

5. The *Cassa per il Mezzogiorno,* literally "The Southern Bank," was a government entity designed to promote and increase economic growth in the South of Italy. It began after World War II.

6. In fact, DiLeonardo disputes the claim that there ever were such things as white ethnic communities. In "Habits of the Cumbered Heart," she says that "American white ethnic populations throughout the nineteenth and twentieth centuries lived in ethnically heterogeneous and shifting urban neighborhoods—and moved often. They also took flight to the suburbs in concert with their urban WASP neighbors. Thus, for example, by the mid-1970s, in the height of white ethnic renaissance publicity, the prototypical California Italian American 'community,' San Francisco's North Beach, had more than 90 percent Chinese residents, and California's Italian American population was in reality scattered far

and wide across the state's urban, suburban, and rural areas" (238). Farr disputes DiLeonardo's claim for Chicago (informal discussion).

7. According to sound ethnographic principles, "Collandia Club" and all other names I use are pseudonyms.

8. According to a history written by a former president, probably in the 1970s, and reprinted in an advertising program booklet created for the celebration of the sixtieth anniversary of the club in 1993.

9. *Ibid.*

10. Sereni refers to immigration as the *"espressione identaria della Lucchesitá"* (the expression of Lucchese identity) (36).

11. In his discussion of Milwaukee Italian "formal voluntary associations," Andreozzi categorizes four goals typically mentioned in charter statements of purpose:

1) desire for acculturation and civic assimilation;
2) desirability of pan-Italianism and its potential for political power;
3) need for economic activity beyond the scope of the traditional mutual aid benefits;
4) desire to sponsor social, recreational, and entertainment activities.

It would seem that the Collandia is interested in all four.

12. See Pozzetta for a wonderful summary of Italian American research including religion and ethnicity, the migration experience itself, and Italian social mobility.

13. For these authors' works (and many others) I thank the Immigration History Research Center at the University of Minnesota where I spent a lovely week in March of 1997 reading papers on Italian immigration.

14. See "Giving an Altar to St. Joseph" for a feminist interpretation of this folklore/performance.

15. Rogers describes a peasant society in Northeastern France in which both men and women pretend that the men are dominant. In this way, men have the satisfaction of appearing important while women make most of the real decisions. Because the domestic unit was the most important economic unit in this society, and the women controlled the domestic unit, it was to everyone's advantage to behave as if males were dominant. The system would break down if this delicate balance of female power and male prestige were not maintained by both sexes.

16. The twenty-five-year-old in question, a daughter of a member, petitioned for membership because she wanted to join the bocce team. A special (men's) board meeting was held where her membership was approved with the proviso that if she marries, she may only retain membership if her husband is approved for membership and joins.

17. In a conversation about powerful female figures, Marcia Farr supplied the term "honorary Italian," which has been useful in my understanding of the monolingual Ladies' Club President's role.

18. This appropriate description comes from David Seitz.

19. Gabaccia comes to a similar conclusion about her Siciliani from Sambuca: "Aware of the differences separating them from the people they called 'Americans,' immigrant Sicilians saw in cultural change a threat to their identity" (*From Sicily to Elizabeth Street* 116). So does Bianco, who says about her Italian-immigrant town of Roseto in Pennsylvania: ". . . individuals are—consciously and unconsciously—trying to preserve certain traditional values, once forming the core of their culture of origin" (x). Nelli maintains, on the other hand, that ethnic institutions represent an "important step *away* from old-world patterns" (156), a mixture of Italian and American characteristics.

Chapter 4. Bella Figura *at the Collandia Club*

1. Although Professoressa Harwell points out that in Italian, too, the word "thought" is used in conjunction with gifts, which are sometimes referred to as *pensierini* ("little thoughts").

2. Linked to this issue of "saying 'no' when they mean yes" is the Italian politeness rule called *fare complimenti*, literally "to make compliments." Professoressa Harwell pointed out that Italians of a certain age are enculturated to say "no" before they accept something—an offer of a snack, an honor—simply because it is rude to immediately answer "yes." My Italian sister-in-law, for example, occasionally feels the need to explain my response of "no" to the offer of food or drink. She tells the Italian host or hostess, "*Non fa complimenti*" about me, which means that I do not "make compliments." In other words, my "no" really means "no."

3. See Sensi-Isolani's "Italian Language and Cultural Promotion: The Pitfall of Cross-Cultural Misunderstanding" for a situation that can be largely explicated by an understanding of *bella figura*.

4. See *The Two Madonnas: The Politics of Festival in a Sardinian*

Community for a deconstruction of the political power of *bella figura*. Another venue, but this festival committee operates much like the Collandia Fashion Show committee.

5. Marcia Farr helped me understand indirection as a neutral strategy, rather than as a manipulative one. When I was trying to make sense of how the women's power seemed–at the same time–so strong and so underneath the surface, this apparent dichotomy puzzled me.

Conclusion

1. See my "Is It True Love or Not?: Patterns of Ethnicity and Gender in Nancy Savoca"; also, my "*A Trip to Barga*" in *Travelers' Tales: Italy*.

2. For a detailed history of the feminist movement in Italy, see Chiavola Birbaum; for an interesting version linking feminism and identity, see Anna Camaiti-Hostert.

3. In Italy, a country where motherhood is so highly prized, it is not surprising that feminists have linked the *affidamento* to the nurturing mother-daughter bond, which is its precursor.

4. For accounts of all ethnographies as "fictions," see Van Maanen, Clifford and Marcus, Renato Rosaldo, among others.

Works Cited

Andreozzi, John. "*Contadini* and *Pescatori* in Milwaukee: Assimilation and Voluntary Associations." Unpublished Masters thesis, University of Wisconsin at Milwaukee, 1974.

Andreucci, Franco. "Modern Italy: 1860 to the Present." *History, Art, and the Genius of a People: The Italians*. Ed. John Julius Norwich. New York: Harry N. Abrams, 1983. 219–253.

Balancio, Dorothy Marie Cali. "The Making and Unmaking of a Myth: Italian American Women and their Community." Unpublished Ph.D. Dissertation, City University of New York, 1985.

Baroja, Julio Caro. "Honour and Shame: A Historical Account of Several Conflicts." *Honor and Shame: The Values of Mediterranean Society*. Ed. J. G. Peristiany. London: University of Chicago Press, 1966. 79–137.

Barolini, Helen, ed. *The Dream Book: An Anthology of Writings by Italian American Women*. New York: Schocken Books, 1987.

Barolini, Helen. Personal Correspondence. June, 1992.

Barzini, Luigi. *The Italians: A Full-Length Portrait Featuring Their Manners and Morals*. New York: Atheneum, 1964.

Bauman, Richard. *Verbal Art as Performance*. Prospect Heights, Il: Waveland Press, 1977.

Bauman, Richard and Joel Sherzer, eds. *Explorations in the Ethnography of Speaking*. Cambridge: Cambridge University Press, 1974.

Belenky, Mary Field, Blythe McVicker Clinchy, Nancy Rule Goldberger, and Jill Mattuck Tarule. *Women's Ways of Knowing: The Development of Self, Voice and Mind*. New York: Basic, 1986.

Berger, Bennett M. Foreword. *Frame Analysis*. By Erving Goffman. New York: Harper and Row, 1974. xi–xviii.

Bernard, Jessie. "Reviewing the Impact of Women's Studies on Sociology." *The Impact of Feminist Research in the Academy*. Ed. Christie Farnham. Bloomington: Indiana University Press, 1987. 193–216.

Bianco, Carla. *The Two Rosetos*. Bloomington: Indiana University Press, 1974.

Birnbaum, Lucia Chiavola. *Liberazione della Donna: Feminism in Italy*. Middleton, Conn: Wesleyan University Press, 1986.

Bodine, Ann. "Androcentrism in Prescriptive Grammar." *Language in Society* 4 (1975): 129–146.

Bonaccorsi, Marisa. Informal discussions with author, Chicago, Illinois. 1991–1997.

Bonora, Ettore. *Presentazione. Il Libro del Cortegiano.* By Baldassare Castiglione. Milano: Gruppo Ugo Mursia Editore, S.p.A., 1972. 5–13.

Bourdieu, Pierre. *A Social Critique of the Judgement of Taste.* Trans. Richard Nice. Cambridge, Mass.: Harvard University Press, 1984.

Brandes, Stanley. "Reflections on Honor and Shame in the Mediterranean." *Honor and Shame and the Unity of the Mediterranean.* Ed. David D. Gilmore. Washington,D.C.: The American Anthropological Association, 1987. 121–134.

Brettell, Caroline B. and Patricia A. deBerjeois. "Anthropology and the Study of Immigrant Women." *Seeking Common Ground: Multidisciplinary Studies of Immigrant Women in the United States.* Ed. Donna Gabaccia. Westport, Conn: Greenwood Press, 1992. 41–63.

Briggs, Charles L. *Competence in Performance: The Creativity of Tradition in Mexicano Verbal Art.* Philadelphia: University of Penn, 1988.

Brown, Penelope. "How and Why are Women More Polite: Some Evidence from a Mayan Community." *Women and Language in Literature and Society.* Eds. Sally McConnell-Ginet, Ruth Borker, and Nelly Furman. New York: Praeger Publishers, 1980. 111–136.

Bull, George. Introduction. *The Book of the Courtier.* By Baldesar Castiglione. London: Penquin Books, 1967.

Burckhardt, Jacob. *The Civilization of the Renaissance in Italy.* New York: The Modern Library, 1954.

Burke, Peter. *The Fortunes of the Courtier: The European Reception of Castiglione's Cortegiano.* University Park, Pa: The Pennsylvania State University Press, 1995.

———. *Popular Culture in Early Modern Europe.* NY: New York University Press, 1978.

Calcagno, Giorgio, ed. *Bianco, Rosso e Verde: L'Identitá degli Italiani.* Roma-Bari: Editori Laterza, 1993.

Calendario Atlante De Agostini 1994. Stampa Officine Graphiche De Agostini: Novara, Italy, 1993.

Camaiti-Hostert, Anna. *"Passing": Dissolvere le Identitá, Superare le Differenze.* Roma: Castelvecchi, 1996.

Cameron, Deborah, ed. *The Feminist Critique of Language: A Reader.* London: Routledge, 1990.

Candeloro, Dominic. "Chicago's Italians: A Survey of the Ethnic Factor 1850–1985." *Ethnic Chicago: A Multicultural Portrait.* Eds. Melvin

G. Holli and Peter d'A. Jones. Grand Rapids, Mi: William B. Eerdmans Publishing Co, 1995. 229–259.

Casillo, Robert. "Moments in Italian-American Cinema: From Little Caesare to Coppola and Scorsese." *From the Margin: Writings in Italian Americana.* Eds. A. J. Tamburri, P.A. Giordano, and F. L. Gardaphe. Purdue University Press, 1991. 374–396.

Castiglione, Baldassare. *The Book of the Courtier.* 1528. Trans. Sir Thomas Hoby. London: J.M. Dent and Sons Ltd., 1994.

Chodorow, Nancy. *The Reproduction of Mothering: Psychoanalysis and the Sociology of Gender.* Berkeley: University of California Press, 1978.

Cinel, Dino. *From Italy to San Francisco: The Immigrant Experience.* Stanford University Press, 1982.

Clifford, James and George E. Marcus, eds. *Writing Culture: The Poetics and Politics of Ethnography.* Berkeley: University of California Press, 1986.

Coates, Jennifer and Deborah Cameron, eds. *Women in Their Speech Communities.* London: Longman, 1988.

Cornelisen, Ann. *Women of the Shadows.* New York: Vintage Books, 1976.

Covello, Leonard. *The Social Background of the Italo-American School Child.* Leiden, Netherlands: E. J. Brill, 1967.

Cox, Virginia. Introduction. *The Book of the Courtier.* 1528. Trans. Sir Thomas Hoby. London: J.M. Dent and Sons Ltd., 1994. xvii–xxxi.

Del Negro, Giovanna. E-mail communication with author. May, 1997.

Del Negro, Giovanna. "'Our Little Paris': Gender, Popular Culture and the Promenade in Central Italy." Unpublished Ph.D. Dissertation, Indiana University, 1998.

Di Leonardo, Micaela. "The Female World of Cards and Holidays: Women, Families, and the Work of Kinship." *Signs: Journal of Women in Culture and Society* 12, 3 (1987): 440–453.

———. "Habits of the Cumbered Heart: Ethnic Community and Women's Culture as American Invented Traditions." *Golden Ages, Dark Ages: Imagining the Past in Anthropology and History.* Eds. William Roseberry and Jay O'Brien. University of California Press, 1991. 234–252.

———. *The Varieties of Ethnic Experience: Kinship, Class, and Gender among California Italian-Americans.* Ithaca and London: Cornell University Press, 1984.

Eckert, Penelope. "Sound Change and Adolescent Social Structure." *Language in Society* 17 (1988): 183–207.

Eckert, Penelope and Sally McConnell-Ginet. "Communities of practice: Where language, gender, and power all live." Kira Hall, Mary Bucholtz, and Birch Moonwomon, eds. *Locating Power: Proceedings of the Second Berkeley Women and Language Conference, April 4 & 5, 1992.* Berkeley: University of California. 89–99.

Edwards, Viv. "The Speech of British Black Women in Dudley, West Midlands." *Women in Their Speech Communities.* Eds. Jennifer Coates and Deborah Cameron. London and New York: Longman, 1988. 33–50.

Eyewitness Travel Guides: Florence and Tuscany. London: Dorling Kindersley Limited, 1994.

Faigley, Lester, *Fragments of Rationality: Postmodernity and the Subject of Composition.* Pittsburgh and London: University of Pittsburg Press, 1992.

Farr, Marcia. "*Echando Relajo*: Verbal Art and Gender Among *Mexicanas* in Chicago." *Proceedings of the Berkeley Women and Language Conference.* University of California, Berkeley: Department of Linguistics, April, 1994.

———. Informal Discussions with author, Chicago, Illinois. 1991–95.

Fasold, Ralph. *The Sociolinguistics of Language.* Oxford: Blackwell Publishers, 1990.

Fishman, Pamela. "Interaction: The Work Women Do." *Social Problems* 24 (1978): 397–406.

Fontanesi, L. and I. Ugolotti. *L'Universo Della Parola: Corso di Educazione Linguistica.* Bergamo: Minerva Italica, 1983.

Foster, George. "Peasant Society and the Image of Limited Good." *American Anthropologist* 67 (April 1965).

Gabaccia, Donna. *From Sicily to Elizabeth Street: Housing and Social Change Among Italian Immigrants, 1880–1930.* Albany, NY: State University of New York Press, 1984.

———. *Seeking Common Ground: Multidisciplinary Studies of Immigrant Women in the United States.* Westport, Conn: Greenwood Press, 1992.

Gal, Susan. "Peasant Men Can't Get Wives: Language Change and Sex Roles in a Bilingual Community." *Language in Society* 7 (1978): 1–16.

Gardaphe, Fred L. *Italian Signs, American Streets: The Evolution of Italian American Narrative.* Durham, N.C.: Duke University Press, 1996.

Geertz, Clifford. "Thick Description: Toward an Interpretive Theory of Culture." *The Interpretation of Cultures.* Ed. Cliford Geertz. New York: Basic Books, Inc., 1973. 3–30.

Gilligan, Carol. *In A Different Voice*. Cambridge: Harvard University Press, 1982.

Gilmore, David D. "Introduction: The Shame of Dishonor." *Honor and Shame and the Unity of the Mediterranean*. Ed. David D. Gilmore. Washington, D.C.: The American Anthropological Association, 1987. 2–21.

Ginsborg, Paul, ed. *Stato dell'Italia*. Milano: Il Saggiatore/Mondadori, 1994.

Giovannini, Maureen J. "Female Chastity Codes in the Circum-Mediterranean: Comparative Perspectives." *Honor and Shame and the Unity of the Mediterranean*. Ed. David D. Gilmore. Washington, D. C.: The American Anthropological Association, 1987. 61–74.

Goffman, Erving. *Frame Analysis*. New York: Harper and Row, 1974.

———. *The Presentation of Self in Everyday Life*. New York: Anchor Books, 1959.

Goodwin, Marjorie Harness. "Directive-Response Speech Sequences in Girls' and Boys' Task Activities." *Women and Language in Literature and Society*. Eds. Sally McConnell-Ginet, Ruth Borker, and Nelly Furman. New York: Praeger Publishers, 1980. 157–173.

———. *He-Said-She-Said: Talk as Social Organization among Black Children*. Bloomington: Indiana University Press, 1990.

Graddol, David and Joan Swann. *Gender Voices*. Oxford: Basil Blackwell, 1989.

Grande Dizionario Hazon Garzanti: Inglese/Italiano Italiano/Inglese. Ed. Mario Hazon. Milano: Garzanti, 1988.

Gumperz, John J. *Discourse Strategies*. Cambridge: Cambridge University Press, 1982.

Hall, Kira, Mary Bucholtz, and Birch Moonwomon, eds. *Locating Power: Proceedings of the Second Berkeley Women and Language Conference, April 4 & 5, 1992* . Berkeley: University of California Press.

Harding, Susan. "Women and Words in a Spanish Village." *Toward an Anthropology of Women*. Ed. Rayna R. Reiter. New York: Monthly Review Press, 1975.

Harwell, Margherita Pieracci. Informal discussions with author, Chicago, Illinois. 1992–94.

Heilman, Judith Adler. *Journeys among Women: Feminism in Five Italian Cities*. New York and Oxford: Oxford University Press, 1987.

Herzfeld, Michael. " 'As in Your Own House': Hospitality, Ethnography and the Stereotype of Mediterranean Society." *Honor and Shame and the Unity of the Mediterranean*. Ed. David D. Gilmore.

Wash, DC: The American Anthropological Association, 1987. 75–89.

Hymes, Dell. "The Ethnography of Speaking." *Anthropology and Human Behavior.* Eds. T. Gladwin and W. Sturtevant. Washington, D.C.: Anthropological Society of Washington, 1962. 15–53.

———. *Foundations in Sociolinguistics: An Ethographic Approach.* Philadelphia: University of Pennsylvania Press, 1974.

Jeffries, Giovanna Miceli, ed. *Feminine Feminists: Cultural Practices in Italy.* Minneapolis and London: University of Minnesota Press, 1994.

Kaplan, Robert B. "Cultural Thought Patterns in Inter-Cultural Education." *Language Learning* 6 (1966): 1–20.

Keenan, Elinor, "Norm Makers, Norm Breakers: Uses of Speech by Men and Women in a Malagasy Community." *Explorations in the Ethnography of Speaking.* Eds. Richard Bauman and Joel Sherzer. Cambridge: Cambridge University Press, 1974.

Kennedy, Gavin. *Doing Business Abroad.* New York: Simon and Schuster, 1985.

Labov, William. "The Social Motivation of a Sound Change." *Sociolinguistic Patterns.* Philadelphia: University of Pennsylvania Press, 1972. 3–38.

Lakoff, George and Mark Johnson. *Metaphors We Live By.* Chicago and London: University of Chicago Press, 1980.

Lakoff, Robin. "Language and Woman's Place." *Language in Society* 2(1) (1973): 45–80.

LaPalombara, Joseph. *Democracy Italian Style.* New Haven: Yale University Press: 1987.

Lera, Gugliemo. *Lucca e la sua Provincia.* Lucca: Casa Editrice Lucentia, 1959.

Lindberg, Richard. *Passport's Guide to Ethnic Chicago.* Lincolnwood, Il: Passport Books, 1994.

Lonni, Ada. *Macaroni e Vu' Cumpra': Emigrazione e Immigrazione nella storia della societá italiana.* "Catalogo Supplemento al numero 579 de Il Calendario Del Popolo." Roma: Teti Editore, 1995.

MacDonald, John. "Northern Italians in California, Canada, and Australia." Paper presented at the American Italian Historical Association, Chicago. November 10–12, 1994.

Mc-Connell-Ginet, Sally. "Intonation in a Man's World." *Language, Gender, and Society.* Eds. Barrie Thorne, Chris Kramarae, and Nancy Henley. Cambridge, Mass: Newbury House, 1983.

———. "The Sexual (Re)production of Meaning." *Language, Gender and Professional Writing: Theoretical Approaches and Guidelines for*

Nonsexist Usage. Eds. Francine Wattman Frank and Paula A. Treichler. New York: Modern Language Association, 1989.

Magliocco, Sabina. E-mail correspondence, 5 May, 1997.

Magliocco, Sabina. *The Two Madonnas: The Politics of Festival in a Sardinian Community*. New York: Peter Lang, 1993.

Maltz, Daniel N. and Ruth A. Borker. "A Cultural Approach to Male-Female Communication." *Language and Social Identity*. Ed. John J. Gumperz. Cambridge: Cambridge University Press, 1982.

Mancuso, Arlene. "Women of Old Town." Unpublished Ph.D. Dissertation. Columbia University Teachers' College, 1977.

Marchetti, Giorgio. "*Due o tre cose che si dicono di Lucca.*" *Notizario Lucchesi nel Mondo* 4 (ottobre–dicembre 1996): 19.

Marcus, Michael A. "Horsemen are the Fence of the Land: Honor and History among the Ghiyata of Eastern Morocco." *Honor and Shame and the Unity of the Mediterranean*. Ed. David D. Gilmore. Washington, DC: The American Anthropological Association, 1987. 49–60.

Muraro, Luisa. "*La Politica delle Relazioni.*" ("The Politics of Relationships.") Talk presented at the Conference on European Feminism, University of Chicago, May 16, 1997.

Nardini, Francesco. Informal discussions with author, Chicago, Illinois. 1991–97.

Nardini, Gloria. "*A Trip to Barga.*" *Travelers' Tales: Italy*. Ed. Anne Calcagno, San Francisco: O'Reilly Publishers, 1998. 286.

———. "Is It *True Love* or Not?: Patterns of Ethnicity and Gender in Nancy Savoca." *Voices in Italian Americana*, 2 (1), Spring 1991, 9–17.

Nelli, Humbert S. *Italians in Chicago 1880–1930: A Study in Ethnic Mobility*. New York: Oxford University Press, 1970.

Nichols, Patricia. "Linguistic Options and Choices for Black Women in the Rural South." *Language, Gender, and Society*. Eds. Barrie Thorne, Chris Kramarae, and Nancy Henley. Cambridge, Mass: Newbury House, 1983.

Norwich, John Julius. "Introduction: A Traveller in Italy." *History, Art, and the Genius of a People: The Italians*. Ed. John Julius Norwich. New York: Harry N. Abrams, 1983. 25–30.

Il Nuovo Dizionario Italiano Garzanti. Milano: Garzanti Editore, 1984.

Il Nuovo Vocabulario della Lingua Italiana secondo l'uso di Firenze ordinato dal Ministero della Pubblica Istruzione. Ed. Emilio Broglio et. al. Firenze: M. Cellini, 1897.

Il Nuovo Zingarelli: Vocabulario della Lingua Italiana di Nicola Zingarelli. Eds. Miro Dogliotti e Luigi Rosiello. Bologna: Zanichelli, 1988.

O'Hare, Lynn. <http://made-in-Italy.com/fashion/newsl/lynn/htm>

Pascoli, Giovanni. Inscription on plaque, il Duomo di Barga, Lucca, Italy.

Peristiany, J.G., ed. *Honor and Shame: The Values of Mediterranean Society.* London: University of Chicago Press, 1966.

Pitkin, Donald S. "Italian Urbanscape: Intersection of Private and Public." *The Cultural Meaning of Urban Space.* Eds. Robt Rotenberg and Gary McDonogh. Westport, Conn: Bergin and Garvey, 1993. 95–101.

Pitt-Rivers, Julian. "Honour and Social Status." *Honor and Shame: The Values of Mediterranean Society.* Ed. J. G. Peristiany. London: University of Chicago Press, 1996. 19–77.

Pozzetta, George. "Immigrants and Ethnics: The State of Italian-American Historiography." *Journal of American Ethnic History* (Fall 1989): 67–95.

Radner, Joan N. and Susan S. Lanser. "Strategies of Coding in Women's Cultures." *Feminist Messages: Coding in Women's Folk Cuture.* Ed. Joan Newlon Radner. University of Illinois Press, 1993. 1–29.

Richards, Charles. *The New Italians.* London: Michael Joseph, Ltd., 1994.

Rogers, Susan Carol. "Female Forms of Power and the Myth of Male Dominance: A Model of Female-Male Interaction in Peasant Society." *American Ethnologist* 2 (1975): 727–756.

Romano, Ruggiero. *Paese Italia, Venti Secoli di Identitá.* Rome: Donzelli Editore, 1994.

Rosaldo, Michelle Zimbalist. "Women, Culture and Society: A Theoretical Overview." *Woman, Culture and Society.* Eds. Michelle Zimbalist Rosaldo and Louise Lamphere. Stanford: Stanford University Press, 1974.

Rosaldo, Renato. *Culture and Truth: The Remaking of Social Analysis.* Boston: Beacon Press, 1993.

Salvatorelli, Luigi. *Sommario della storia d'Italia.* Torino: Einaudi, dodicesima edizione, 1969.

Sapegno, Natalino. *Disegno Storico della Letteratura Italiana.* Firenze: La Nuova Italia, 1951.

Saville-Troike, Muriel. *The Ethnography of Communication.* Oxford: Basil Blackwell, Ltd., 1982.

Schellenbaum, Paola. "Stereotypes as Cultural Constructs: A Kaleidoscopic Picture of Italian Americans in Northern California." *Studies in Italian American Folklore.* Ed. Luise Del Giudice. Logan, Utah: Utah State University Press, 1993. 153–202.

Scott, James C. *Domination and the Arts of Resistance: Hidden Transcripts.* New Haven and London: Yale University Press, 1990.

Sensi-Isolani, Paola. "Italian Image Makers in France, England, and the United States." *Italian Americans Celebrate Life: The Arts and Popular Culture.* Eds. Paola A. Sensi Isolani and Anthony Julian Tamburri. Selected Essays from the 22nd Annual Conference of the American Italian Historical Association: 1990, 95–113.

———. "Italian Language and Culture Promotion: The Pitfall of Cross-Cultural Misunderstanding." *Italian Ethnics: Their Languages, Literature and Lives.* Eds. Dominic Candeloro, Fred L. Gardaphe, and Paolo A. Giordano. Proceedings of the 20th Annual Conference of the American Italian Historical Association, 1987, 15–21.

Sereni, Umberto. Introduction: "*Il 'Modello Lucchese.'*" *La Città Industriosa: Lucca alla fine dell'Ottocento.* by Antonio Morosi. Ed. Umberto Sereni. Lucca: Maria Pacini Fazzi Editore, 1997.

Shultz, Jeffrey J., Susan Florio, and Frederick Erickson. "Where's the Floor? Aspects of the Cultural Organization of Social Relationships in Communication at Home and in School." *Children In and Out of School: Ethnography and Education.* Washington, D.C.: The Center for Applied Linguistics. 88–123.

Silverman, Sydel. "Agricultural Organization, Social Structure, and Values in Italy: Amoral Familism Reconsidered." *American Anthropologist* 70 (1968): 1–20.

———. "An Ethnographic Approach to Social Stratification: Prestige in a Central Italian Community." *American Anthropologist* 68 (1966): 899–921.

———. *Three Bells of Civilization: The Life of an Italian Hill Town.* New York and London: Columbia University Press, 1975.

Sollors, Werner. *Beyond Ethnicity: Consent and Descent in American Culture.* New York and Oxford: Oxford University Press, 1986.

Stubbs, Michael. *Discourse Analysis: The Sociolinguistic Analysis of Natural Language.* Chicago: The University of Chicago Press, 1983.

Swann, Joan. "Talk Control: An Illustration from the Classroom of Problems in Analyzing Male Dominance of Conversation." *Women in Their Speech Communities.* Eds. Jennifer Coates and Deborah Cameron. London and New York: Longman, 1988. 123–140.

Tannen, Deborah. "Indirectness in Discourse: Ethnicity as Conversational Style." *Discourse Processes* 4 (1991): 221–238.

Tannen, Deborah. "The Relativity of Linguistic Strategies: Rethinking Power and Solidarity in Gender and Dominance." *Gender and*

Conversational Interaction. Ed. Deborah Tannen. New York and Oxford: Oxford University Press, 1993. 165–88.

———. *Talking Voices: Repetition, Dialogue and Imagery in Conversational Discourse.* Cambridge: Cambridge University Press, 1989.

Thorne, Barrie and Nancy Henley, eds. *Language and Sex: Difference and Dominance.* Rowley, Mass: Newbury House Publishers, 1975.

Thorne, Barrie, Chris Kramarae, and Nancy Henley. *Language, Gender, and Society.* Cambridge, Mass: Newbury House, 1983.

Trudgill, Peter. "Sex, Convert Prestige and Linguistic Change in the Urban British English of Norwich." *Language and Sex: Difference and Dominance.* Eds. Barrie Thorne and Nancy Henley. Roley, Mass: Newbury, 1975. 180–92.

Turner, Kay and Suzanne Seriff. " 'Giving an Altar to St. Joseph': A Feminist Perspective on a Patronal Feast." *Feminist Theory and the Study of Folklore.* Eds. Susan Tower Hollis, Linda Pershing, and M. Jane Young. University of Illinois Press, 1993. 89–117.

Van Maanen, John. *Tales of the Field: On Writing Ethnography.* Chicago and London: University of Chicago Press, 1988.

Vecoli, Rudolph J. "Chicago's Italians Prior to World War I: A Study of their Social and Economic Adjustment." Unpublished Ph.D. Dissertation, University of Wisconsin, 1962.

———. "Contadini in Chicago: A Critique of the Uprooted." *Journal of American History* 51 (Dec 1964): 404–17.

Venturelli, Peter J. "Institutions in an Ethnic District." *Human Organization* 41 (1982): 26–35.

Vocabolario degli accademici della crusca. Firenze: Successori Le Monnier, 1887.

Weinberg, Sydney Stahl. "The Treatment of Women in Immigration History: A Call for Change." *Seeking Common Ground: Multidisciplinary Studies of Immigrant Women in the United States.* Ed. Donna Gabaccia. Westport, Conn: Greenwood Press, 1992. 3–22.

Whorf, Benjamin Lee. *Language, Thought and Reality.* Ed. John B. Carroll. Cambridge: MIT Press, 1956.

Yans-McLaughlin, Virginia. *Family and Community: Italian Immigrants in Buffalo 1880–1930.* Ithaca, N.Y.: Cornell University Press, 1977.

Zimmerman, Don I. and Candace West. "Small Insults: A Study of Interruptions in Cross-Sex Conversations between Unacquainted Persons." *Language, Gender and Society.* Eds. Barrie Thorne, Cheris Kramarae, and Nancy Henely. Rowley, Mass: Newbury, 1983. 103–117.

Index

A

Affidamento. See Italian feminism
"Agricultural Organization, Social Structure, and Values in Italy: Amoral Familism Reconsidered," 17, 43
American dream, 55, 60, 127
Andreozzi, John, 146n. 11
Andreucci, Franco, 29

B

Balancio, Dorothy Marie Cali, 64
Barga, 23, 58
Baroja, Julio Caro, 16
Barolini, Helen, 20, 129
Baroque, 28–29
Barzini, Luigi, 6, 7, 28–29, 32–33
Bauman, Richard, 31–32, 40, 123–24, 127
Bauman and Sherzer, 38
bella figura, 2, 3, 4, 5, 6, 7, 29, 35, 41, 42, 47, 54, 63, 65, 67, 69, 70, 72, 75, 77, 99, 127, 128, 129, 130, 131, 143n. 4 147n. 3; in ancient Rome, 21; Barzini and, 6–7, 32; in *The Book of Courtier*, 22, 24, 27; as central metaphor of Italian life, 7, 10, 30; as code of conduct, 10; Collandia Ladies' Club gift-giving and, 78–80; Collandia Ladies' Club meeting as, 80–86; in contemporary Italy, 12–14; as cultural construct bound to language, 35, 105–25; as display, 11–12, 22–23; dictionary definitions of, 8–10; as display, 11–12, 22–23; dictionary definitions of, 8–10; in Fascism, 29–30; gender issues in, 11, 18; Goffman and 30–32; Harwell's explanation of, 10, 11–14; honor and shame and, 15, 18; "impression management" and, 18; in-

direction in, 3; Italian class system and 13–14; in Italian identity, 20–24; in Italian language, 7–9; in Italian Renaissance, 28; in *lista delle nozze*, 11; literary examples of, 9; in Middle Ages, 22; misunderstandings of, 18–20; as notion of self, 15, 18, 32; Pascoli and, 23–24; *passeggiata* and, 14–15; performance of, 19–21, 27, 30, 31, 32–33, 105–25; popular definitions of, 5–6, 10; power and, 35, 148n. 4; "real rules" of Collandia Ladies' Club and, 87–103; in Roman Baroque, 28; Silverman and, 10–11, 86; spectacle in, 7, 22; *sprezzatura* and, 24–26, 32; understanding of, vii–viii, ix, 3–4, 23; "urbanscape" vs. "inner self" and, 18; verbal art and, 54; "work of kinship" and, 102–3. *See also brutta figura*, Collandia Ladies' Club, *fare bella figura, fare brutta* figura, honor and shame and the values of the Mediterranean, performance, spectacle, *sprezzatura*
Belenky, Mary Field, Blythe McVicker Clinchy, Nancy Rule Goldberger, and Jill Mattuck Tarule, 49
Ber, Mary, x
Berger, Bennett M., 31
Bernard, Jessie, 144n. 2
Bertagni, Norine, ix
Bianco, Carla, 147n. 19
Bianco, Rosso e Verde, L'identitá degli italiani, 143n. 1
Big Night, 129
Bodine, Ann, 48
Bonaccorsi, Marisa, ix, 10

Bonora, Ettore, 25
The Book of the Courtier (Il Cortegiano), 22,
    24, 28; gentlemanly performance in, 27;
    grazia in, 25; *sprezzatura* in, 24–26, 120
Bossi, Umberto, 58
Bourdieu, Pierre, 46–47, 127; *habitus* in,
    101–2
Brandes, Stanley, 16
Brettell, Carolyn and Patricia A. deBer-
    jeois, 6
Briggs, Charles, 40, 127
Brown, Penelope, 48, 53
brutta figura, 6, 8, 9, 11, 13, 18, 19, 29, 30,
    66, 77, 121, 129, 143n. 4, 145n. 1; in-
    direction used to avoid, 99–100, 124;
    losing face and, 83–84; Mussolini and,
    29; *sfigurare* in, 7; traditions and, 82–83,
    84–86; *vergogna* and, 18
Bull, George, 27
"buona" figura, 9
Burckhardt, Jacob, 22–23, 27
Burke, Peter, 7, 17–18, 22, 24, 26, 27

C
Calcagno, Giorgio, 143 n. 1
Calendario Atlante De Agostini 1994, 58
Camaiti-Hostert, Anna, 148n. 1
Cameron, Deborah, 48
campanilismo, 6, 55
Candeloro, Dominick, 55, 60
Cassa per il mezzogiorno, 59, 145n. 5
Casillo, Robert, 18
Castiglione, Baldissare, 22, 24–27, 32, 120
cattiva figura, 8, 143n. 5
Chiavola Birnbaum, Lucia, 148n. 1
"Chicago's Italians: A Survey of the Ethnic
    Factor 1850–1985," 56, 59, 62
Chodorow, Nancy, 49
Cinel, Dino, 59
civiltá, 10, 13, 44–45
clandestini, 6
class, 47, 52–53, 144n. 7; Bourdieu and,
    46–47; contrast between townsman and
    countryman in Silverman and, 43–45;
    as country-specific construct, 42; "real
    rules" of Collandia Ladies' Club and,
    98–103; taste and *habitus* in, 46
Clifford and Marcus, 148n. 3
Coates and Cameron, 48, 52, 53

code-switching, 41, 69, 80, 95, 112, 114
Collandia Club, 3, 4, 35, 54, 55, 60–62,
    63, 64, 65, 66, 69, 70, 71, 73, 74, 75,
    77, 78, 83, 84, 87, 99, 100, 103, 107,
    122, 131, 146n. 7; bylaws of, 63, 97
Collandia Ladies' Club, 1, 48, 64, 65, 66,
    68, 70, 72, 74, 77, 105, 106, 109, 11,
    122, 125, 127; *affidamento* in, 129–30;
    blunders at, 96–98; bocce at, 78; by-
    laws of, 65, 66; bylaws vs. *figura*,
    84–86; celebration of birthdays in,
    77–78; educational background of,
    68–69; "freeloading" and 92–93; gen-
    der issues in, 1; gift-giving and, 78–80;
    as helpers, 87–90; identity in, 127–28;
    indirection in, 95–96; literacy in, 69;
    meetings as performance of *bella figura*,
    80–83, 86; membership make-up of,
    66–68, 94; money and, 90–91; myth of
    gentility in, 70–74; power in, 87; "real
    rules" of, 86–103; social life around,
    69; tradition and, 92–95; typical meet-
    ing of, 65; yearly "affairs" of, 65–66
Colleverde, 13, 44–45
commedia dell'arte, 22
communicative competence, 35, 37, 40,
    47
"community of practice," 53–54, 128
"Contadini in Chicago: A Critique of the
    Uprooted," 59
contadino, 13–14, 59
Coppola, Francis Ford, 144n. 9
Cornelisen, Ann, 64
Il Cortegiano. See *The Book of the Courtier*
Cosa Nostra, 58
Covello, Leonard, 59, 145n. 4
Covino, Bill, x
Cox, Virginia, 25, 28
cultural competence, 37
culture: class and semiotics of language in,
    42, 105; cross-cultural misunderstand-
    ing and, 39, 42, 128; discourse analysis
    and, 124–25; ethnography of commu-
    nication and, 36–37; Geertz and,
    47–48; indirection in, 95–96; language
    codes and, 41–42; performance and,
    38, 39; power and *bella figura* and, 99;
    primacy of, 35; "real rules" of Collan-
    dia Ladies' Club and, 98–103; Sapir-

Whorf hypothesis and, 36; stereotypes of women and, 49

D

Del Negro, Giovanna, 14–15, 18
Democracy Italian Style, 145n. 2
DiLeonardo, Micaela, 52, 102, 145n. 6
Diotima, 129
Discourse Analysis, 39
Disegno Storico della Letteratura Italiana, 27
Doing Business Abroad, 5
Dopo noi, l'Africa!, 145n. 4

E

"*Echando Relajo*: Verbal Art and Gender Among *Mexicanas* in Chicago," 40
Eckert, Penny, 48, 49, 53
Edwards, Viv, 53
ethnicity, 55, 74, 102
"An Ethnographic Approach to Social Stratification: Prestige in a Central Italian Community," 13, 43–45
ethnography of communication, 1–3, 36–37; "thick description" in, 77, 127
Eyewitness Travel Guides, 5
Explorations in the Ethnography of Speaking, 38

F

Faigley, Lester, 128
fare (bella) figura, 5, 7, 9, 12, 14, 33, 35, 41, 47, 75, 82, 99, 102, 103, 127, 132; dictionary definitions of, 8; *figurare* in, 7; *sfigurare* in, 7
fare brutta figura, 8, 11. See also *bella figura; brutta figura; fare bella figura*
fare cattiva figura. See *fare brutta figura*
fare complimenti, 147n. 2
Farr, Marcia, ix, 31, 40, 128, 144n. 8, 146n. 6, 147n. 17, 148n. 5
Fascism, 24, 29
Fasold, Ralph, 36
"The Female World of Cards and Holidays: Women, Families, and the Work of Kinship," 102–3
Feminine Feminists: Cultural Practices in Italy, 129–30
figura. See *bella figura*
figurare. See *bella figura*

figurinai, (image-makers) 62
Fishman, Pamela, 48, 52
Fontanesi and Ugolotti, 7, 143n. 2
Foundations in Sociolinguistics: An Ethnographic Approach, 37
The Fortunes of the Courtier: The European Reception of Castiglione's Cortegiano, 7, 18, 24, 26, 27
Foster, George, 16
Fra Noi, 55
Frame Analysis, 31
From Sicily to Elizabeth Street, 64, 147n. 18

G

Gabaccia, Donna, 64, 147n. 18
Gal, Susan, 48, 50–51
Gardaphe, Fred, x, 19
Geertz, Clifford, 35, 37, 47–48, 105, 124
gender, 74; in *bella figura,* 11, 18; conflicts in Collandia Ladies' Club and, 108; "real rules" of the Collandia Ladies' Club and, 98–103
Gender and Conversational Interaction, 39
Gilligan, Carol, 49–50
Gilmore, David, 16–17, 18
Ginsborg, Paul, 143n. 1
Giovannini, Maureen, 17
"Giving an Alter to St. Joseph," 146n. 14
The Godfather, 19
Goffman, Erving, 30–33, 38, 77, 111, 127
Gonzaga, Cesare, 26
Goodwin, Marjorie, 48, 50
Graddol and Swann, 48
Grande Dizionario Hazon Garzanti: Inglese-Italiano, Italiano-Inglese, 8
grazia, 25; in *The Book of the Courtier,* 25; in English, 25; in Italian definitions, 25–26; observable as *sprezzatura,* 26–27
Gumperz, John, 39, 40–41, 127

H

"Habits of the Cumbered Heart: Ethnic Community and Women's Culture as American Invented Traditions," 145–46n. 6
habitus. See Bourdieu
Harding, Susan, 48, 49
Harwell, Professor Margherita Pieracci, ix, 10–14, 22, 144n. 7, 147n. 1, 147n. 2

He-Said-She-Said, 50
Heilman, Judith Adler, 62
Herzfeld, Michael, 16–17
The History of the Collandia Ladies' Club by Gloria Nardini, 70–72; deconstruction of the myth and, 72–74
Hoby, Sir Thomas, 24
Honor and Shame and the Unity of the Mediterranean, 16
honor and shame and the values of Mediterranean society, 15; *bella figura* and, 18; Brandes and, 16; female chastity codes in, 16; Gilmore and, 16; Herzfeld and, 16; Marcus and, 16; *vergogna* in, 16
Hull House, 55
Hymes, Dell, 36–37, 105

I
immigration, 55–56, 58–60, 64, 101, 129, 146n. 10, 145n. 13; *rimesse degli emigrati* in, 62
Immigration History Research Center, ix, 146n. 13
indirection. See *bella figura*; Collandia Ladies' Club; culture; language; "myth of male dominance;" power
"Indirectness in Discourse: Ethnicity as Conversational Style," 39
"Is It True Love or Not: Patterns of Ethnicity and Gender in Nancy Savoca," 148n. 6
Italian class system, 13; *rispetto* and, 42
Italian feminism, 3; *affidamento* in, 129–30, 148n. 1, 148n. 2
Italian identity, 6, 21; in *bella figura*, 20; display of collective in, 122; importance of ceremony in Middle Ages to, 21; in piazza artistry, 22–23; by regions, 56–58, 59–60; in Renaissance, 22; in Romans, 21
"Italian Language and Culture Promotion: The Pitfall of Cross-Cultural Misunderstanding," 147n. 3
Italian Renaissance, 22, 27, 28, 58
The Italians: A Full-Length Portrait Featuring Their Manners and Morals, 6
Italy: 1948 constitution of, 56; map of, 57; 20 regions of, 56–58

Italy, Central, 10, 17, 43, 57–58, 60, 62, 144n. 2, 145n. 3, 145n. 4; *rispetto* and *civiltá* in, 45; urban traditions in, 10
Italy, Northern, 57–58, 59, 60, 70, 74–75, 145n. 3, 145n. 4; divisions between Southern Italy and, 58
Italy, Southern, 17, 43, 57–58, 145n. 3, 145n. 4; "problem" of, 58–59; "special" moral code of, 59

J
Jeffries, Giovanna Miceli, 129
Judd, Elliot, 143n. 4

K
Kaplan, Robert B., 143n. 2
Keenan, Elinor, 48, 52
Kennedy, Gavin, 5
Kohlberg scale of moral development, 49, 144n. 3

L
La Lega, 58
Labov, William, 41, 50, 53
Lakoff, Robin, 48
Lakoff and Johnson, 7, 29–30
Ladies' Club. *See* Collandia Ladies' Club; women
La Motta, Jake, 18–19
language: in bilingual, bicultural context, 35, 40–41, 121–22; class and, 42; code-switching and, 41; at Collandia Ladies' Club meetings, 93–95, 99; communicative strategies in, 122–23; cultural codes and, 41; cultural imbeddedness of, 35, 37, 105; gender and, 48–54, 110–11; potential for cross-cultural misunderstanding and, 42; powerless vs. powerful, 112–22; relationship with culture, 42; Sapir-Whorf hypothesis and, 36; speech community in, 36; transformation by *bella figura* and, 105–25; women's, 53
LaPalombara, Joseph, 145n. 2, 145n. 4
Lave, Jean and Wenger, Etienne, 53
Lazzerini, Augustus J., ix
Lazzerini, Joan, ix
Lera, Gugliemo, 62
"limited good," 16

Lindberg, Richard, 60
lista delle nozze (bridal registry), 11
Locating Power: Proceedings of the Second Berkeley Women and Language Conference, 48
Lonni, Ada, 60
Lucca, 23, 57–58, 59, 60, 68, 75, 87, 107, 127, 144n. 2
lucchese/i, 3, 56, 58, 62, 68, 75, 107, 146n. 10

M
MacDonald, John, 60
McConnell-Ginet, Sally, 48, 53
McCormick Reaper Works, 56, 74
Mafia, 55, 59, 60, 145n. 1
Magliocco, Sabina, x, 145n. 4
Maltz, Daniel N. and Ruth A. Borker, 48
Mancuso, Arlene, 64
Manzoni, Alessandro, 9
Marchetti, Giorgio, 62
Marcus, Michael, 16
Menotti, Gian Carlo, 144n. 9
Men's Club. *See* Collandia Club
methodology. *See* ethnography of communication
Mirabella, Grace, 144n. 9
miseria, (extreme poverty) 56
Moffo, Anna, 144n. 9
Morrison, Toni, 131
Muraro, Luisa, 3
Mussolini, 29
"myth of male dominance," 68, 100, 103

N
National Malleable Grant Works, 56
Nardini, Francesco, 10
Nardini, Gian Carlo, ix, 129
Nardini, Guido, ix
Nazi Germany, 29
Nelli, Humbert S., 147n. 19
Nichols, Patricia, 48, 50–51
nomi alterati, 7
Northwest Terra Cotta Works, 56
Norwich, John Julius, 5
Il Nuovo Dizionario Italiano Garzanti, 8
Il Nuovo Vocabolario della Lingua Italiana, 8, 9
Il Nuovo Zingarelli, 25–26, 130

O
O'Hare, Lynn, 6
omertá, (silence before public officials) 59
" 'Our Little Paris': Gender, Popular Culture and the Promenade in Central Italy," 15
The Oxford English Dictionary, 20–21

P
Paese Italia, Venti Secoli di identitá, 6, 143n. 1
Pascoli, Giovanni, 23
passeggiata (promenade), 14–15
Passport's Guide to Ethnic Chicago, 60
Peters, Bernadette, 144n. 9
performance: Barzini and, 32–33; in Richard Bauman, 31–32, 40; Bauman and Sherzer and, 38; of *bella figura,* 32, 41–42, 80–86, 97, 105–25; bilinguals and, 40–41; in *The Book of the Courtier,* 27; as communally constructed, 123–35; culturally coded meanings in, 39–40; definitions of, 20–21; in Marcia Farr, 31; Goffman and, 30–32, 38; in Italian festivals, 22–23; indirection in, 97–98; power and, 40; presentation of self and, 38
Peristiany, J.G., 15, 16
Pitkin, Donald, 15, 18, 20
Pitt-Rivers, Julian, 15
Popular Culture in Early Modern Europe, 18, 22
power: culture and *fare bella figura* and, 99; linguistic use of *bella figura* and, 105–25; "real rules" of Collandia Ladies' Club and, 98–103. *See also bella figura*; performance
Pozzetta, George, 64, 146n. 12
The Presentation of Self in Everyday Life, 30–31, 38
Il Progresso Italo-Americano, 55
I Promessi Sposi, 9

R
Radner, Joan N. and Susan S. Lanser, 53
Raging Bull, 18
"The Relativity of Linguistic Strategies: Rethinking Power and Solidarity in Gender and Dominance," 99
Richards, Charles, 5

rispetto (prestige), 42, 45
Robert's Rules of Order, 65
Rogers, Susan Carol, 68, 99–100, 102,
    146n. 15
Romano, Ruggiero, 6, 21, 143n. 1
Rome, 56, 57; ancient, 6, 21; Baroque, 28;
    Fascist, 29
Rosaldo, Michelle Zimbalist, 48, 49
Rosaldo, Renato, 148n. 3
Rushdie, Salman, 7

S
Salvatorelli, Luigi, 28, 29
Sapegno, Natalino, 27
Sapir-Whorf hypothesis, 36
Saville-Troike, Muriel, 37, 41, 105, 106;
    composition of scene in, 106–7; mes-
    sage form and content in, 109; norms
    of interpretation in, 110; rules for in-
    teraction in, 109–10
Scavullo, Francesco, 144n. 9
Schellenbaum, Paola, 75
Scott, James C., 53
*Seeking Common Ground: Multidisciplinary
    Studies of Immigrant Women in the United
    States*, 64
Seitz, David, 147n. 18
Sensi-Isolani, Paola, 62
Sereni, Umberto, 143n. 1, 146n. 10
sfigurare, 7. See also *brutta figura*
Shultz, Florio and Erickson, 144n. 1
Sicily, 17, 56, 56, 59, 64
Silverman, Sydel, 10, 13, 17, 42–46, 122,
    144n. 2
*The Social Background of the Italo-American
    School Child*, 145n. 4
A Social Critique of the Judgment of Taste, 46
Sollors, Werner, 67
spectacle, 6, 22, 125, 144n. 2
sprezzatura, 24–27, 32–33, 120
St. Joseph's Day, 65, 72, 74, 91, 100
Stubbs, Michael, 39, 105, 110, 124, 127
Swann, Joan, 52

T
*Talking Voices: Repetition, Dialogue and Im-
    agery in Conversational Discourse*, 39,
    120, 123

Tannen, Deborah, 38–39, 99, 105, 120,
    122, 123, 144n. 1
Thorne, Barrie and Nancy Henley, 48
Thorne, Barrie, Chris Kramarae, and
    Nancy Henley, 48
*Three Bells of Civilization: The Life of an
    Italian Hill Town*, 11, 44, 86, 122,
    144n. 2
Toscana (Tuscany), 57, 58, 62, 144n. 2
"A Trip to Barga," 148n. 6
Trudgill, Peter, 48, 50, 51
True Love, 129
*The Two Madonnas: The Politics of Festival in
    a Sardinian Community,* 148n. 5

U
Umbertina, 20
L'universo della parola, 143n. 2
The Untouchables, 55
urban traditions, 10, 43

V
Van Maanen, John, 148n. 3
Vecoli, Rudolph, 56, 59, 62
Venturelli, Joseph, 74–75
Verbal Art as Performance, 124
vergogna, 16, 18
Il Vocabolario degli accademici della crusca, 9

W
Weinberg, Sydney, 64
women: identity and, 50–51; in immigra-
    tion, 64–65; institutionalized sexism
    and, 52; gossip and, 49, 52; "moral au-
    thority" and, 49; social context of lan-
    guage and, 50; as subordinate group,
    53. See also Collandia Ladies' Club;
    women's language studies
women's language studies, 48–54
"the work of kinship," 102–3

Y
Yans-McLaughlin, Virginia, 64

Z
Zimmerman, Don and Candace West, 48,
    52